"Becky's book, "Hidden in Plain Sight" is a beautiful and personal work filled with passages I read over and over again to let them penetrate my heart with their gentle invitation to ponder my life and my ever pursuing God. It is a golden read and one that resonates with and lingers in the heart. Read it and find out for yourself!"

Stasi Eldredge, is a teacher and conference speaker.
She is author of Becoming Myself and coauthor of
Captivating and Love and War with her husband, John.

"Dysfunction is in our DNA from the fall. All of us grew up in imperfect homes and we fail to create that ideal home we imagine. Our failure is actually a gift because it reveals the God-created longing for our True Home. My friend Becky bravely and wisely shares her life stories to show any reader what redemption, hope and anticipation look like. Reading her words will inspire your own hope and brave anticipation for what only God can do today and one day in our new Home!"

Barbara Rainey, Author of Letters to My Daughters, The
Art of Being a Wife, and founder of EverThineHome, a blog
and product line for women. everthinehome.com.

"In reading Becky's story you will hear echoes of your own story. You too will realize that you are not invisible. Her rich chapter questions will enable you to celebrate your own uniqueness."

Susan Alexander Yates, speaker and author of <u>Risky Faith.</u>

"My wise friend Becky has a quiet, compelling voice. When she speaks, you lean in to hear, to gather the pearls that tumble softly from her lips. You will want to lean in to this written strand of stories. Becky kindly shares her treasure and gently urges us to explore our own stories to discover the hidden gems in plain sight. As we enter this trove of story wisdom, we will engage more deeply with the Author who has written redemption into our very own hearts."

Elizabeth Reynolds Turnage, Writer, Story Coach, Teacher

"Becky Allender lives well. And thoughtfully. And bravely. And — lucky us! — this woman can write. Her stories invite us into our own stories, encouraging us to contemplate what future stories *we* might write (and live) out of our own unique past journeys, both heartbreaking and glorious."

Cary Umhau, Author of Burning Down the Fireproof Hotel

Hidden In
Plain Sight

Dear Cathy

Because of you – your brilliance
and your beauty – this
book exists. Thank you is not
a big enough word ...

But still I say thank you.
Your sentence to me, "You
have a gift (my writing) spurred
me on.

May this book lead to a
greater kindness to yourself.

Love,

Becky

Hidden In Plain Sight

ONE WOMAN'S SEARCH FOR IDENTITY, INTIMACY AND CALLING

Becky Allender

BlueWing
PRESS

For more information, address:

Blue Wing Press
P.O. Box 11438
Bainbridge Island, WA 98110

Published 2017 by Blue Wing Press

Printed in the United States of America

ISBN: 1947974009

ISBN: 9781947974005

Library of Congress Control Number: 2017914931

Cover design by Sheila Cowley

Front and back cover photos by Jeff Christian

To my grandchildren Cole, Van, Elsa, Grace, and August:
I love how your lives shape mine, and I pray that
my life will always be part of yours.

Acknowledgments

I now understand the frustration actors feel trying to thank a host of people in a matter of minutes. No one wants an Academy Award–winner's acceptance speech to go on for long, but brevity denies recognizing the scores of instruments that made up the symphony.

I am thankful for Amy Anderson and her persistence that got me to travel to a week long training called The Journey Open Hearts.

I am appreciative of Red Tent Living for giving me the privilege of launching my voice. Tracy Johnson, thank you for not accepting my check to help launch Red Tent Living and asking me to write instead. I couldn't have been more surprised, and without your invitation this book wouldn't have been written.

Countless friends, particularly Jane Barry, Laurie Proctor, Cathy Loerzel, Jen Murphy, Laura Wade Shirley, Linda Busse, Annie Klein, Stasi Eldredge, and Cary Umhau, who repeatedly said, "You need to write a book!" Your encouragement has been a haunting gift I've needed to keep moving forward.

To Traci Mullins: How sweet it is that you launched my husband's first few books and have been the gracious midwife who helped birth my first labor. Your gifts and kindness have been indispensable.

To Jennifer Lonas: I thought I was finished with my book, but your sharp editing eyes gave me so much more needed clarity. I will never forget your care and skillful guidance on the final stretch of this marathon.

To my friends and colleagues at the Allender Center: How odd it is that I've come to find my voice and joy through an organization that bears my last name. You know only too well how you've honored me, called me to address trauma and abuse in my story, and invited me to use my gifts for others. I'm eternally grateful.

To my children, Annie, Amanda, and Andrew, and to your spouses, Driscoll, Jeff, and Elizabeth—there isn't a moment of life or a moment of writing when your faces are forgotten. The joy you bring is the crown of my life.

To my husband, Dan: Words will never be able to express my gratitude for your care and delight in me. Your heart of kindness has caused me to see the bounty of gifts God gives to me daily. Like a river, you are an endless source of life that is forever changing and forever the same. Our efforts to speak our love to each other are countless, and I can only say publicly again, I love you, I love you, I love you. I cannot imagine journeying on this earth without you by my side. You are my life.

Contents

Foreword

I remember the exact moment when I realized that my wife is a writer. Some awareness came before we were married. We were apart for the first year of our relationship and we wrote daily. I prized the letters. The descriptions of her daily life enthralled me. Indeed, I was madly in love and that kind of madness doesn't offer the best lens for aesthetic judgement. Her words have moved my heart for over 40 years. But that is a personal communion, not necessarily a commendation of her craft of writing.

I remember reading one of her articles on a plane. I was sitting in 21 D, an exit row. I recall the woman sitting next to me and her lap was laden with a laptop, book, sewing project and headphones. As I read Becky's writing, I began to cry. I knew the situation she was describing. I had been with her, but there was something about what she wrote that enabled me to see what occurred in a different light. But even more than that she gave me words to describe what I had refused to feel. She did so with fierce honesty and kindness.

The more I read, the more I wept. My shirt sleeve served as the best means to dry my tears. As I read to the end, I felt something slight land on my leg. I looked down and it was a Kleenex that came without a word or a look from the angel sitting to my right. I think it was at that propitious moment that I said out loud: "My wife is a writer."

What you will discover in this book is a woman who knows what it is like to live in the shadows and has chosen to let the sunlight highlight her beauty to reveal the goodness of the One who created her. I am biased, of course. Yet, I believe this book will enable you to take more seriously the goodness of your life, the power of your stories, and the wonder of giving your story away.

Dan B. Allender, Ph.D.
Bainbridge Island, Washington
October 2, 2017

Preface

My husband has said many times, "We don't just have stories; we are our stories." In the pages that follow, you'll read thirty-four brief glimpses into my life, stories that have shaped my identity, drawn me toward intimacy, and defined my calling. And there are thousands more I could share with you!

We are all on a quest for identity, intimacy, and calling. Your own life is filled with countless experiences and significant events that have shaped you as a person. These are your stories! You may have shared some of these stories with others, while choosing to keep some private, hidden out of sight because of fear or shame. Many stories may be lost to conscious memory because you haven't given them a place to live and breathe.

My hope for you, dear reader, as you listen to the stories in this book is that you will learn to recognize the voice of your own stories. I want you to remember them, ponder them. Let them "breathe" and allow them to speak about your life, your dreams, your losses, and your joys.

As you let your stories have a voice, you may find they have a life of their own, stories to tell that you haven't heard before. Listen to these stories and learn from them.

At the end of each essay, I'll ask you to recall a personal story that reflects one of the themes in the essay and write about it in your journal. Then I'll invite you to ponder a few questions. Reflect, listen, and write. And then write some more. As you describe the scene, characters, time, plot, and outcome of your story, you might just hear a voice beckoning you to open your heart to the Author of all our stories.

In the writing of your story, you'll be preparing a beautiful gift for your family and friends and the greatest legacy your children will ever receive! Let my stories inspire you to tell your own!

Introduction

When I was a newlywed, one of the things I asked for one Christmas was the wooden box my mother-in-law's relatives stored their tools in when they emigrated from Germany in the early 1800s. I've used it in various ways over the years, but when my husband, Dan, and I had grandchildren, it took on a new role as the designated treasure chest.

Allender Family Chest, circa 1800

Whenever our grandchildren come to our home, before reaching the front door, they shout, "Can we go see what's in the treasure chest?" My hope is that in years to come, they will recall those moments of discovery in a way that forever makes them feel connected to their Mia and Papa even after we are gone.

My husband and I were on a walk yesterday, and we talked about how quickly the years are flying by. We used to walk these same streets when our children were young, and now they have moved away and have children of their own. I vividly remember my grandparents, and now Dan and I are the grandparents! I wish I had asked my grandma and granddaddy so many more questions about their lives. I wish they had told me more stories of their childhoods and young-adult years. It seems that when we're young, we have little time to listen to the stories of previous generations and little understanding of their value. Curiosity often comes after our grandparents and parents have passed away. By the time our children want to hear our stories, many of us may no longer be living.

When my parents died, they each left, to my surprise, diaries of their young-adult years, "hidden" in plain sight. When I discovered them in the closet, I gasped as I reached for the leather-bound books my parents had written so long ago. What a treasure! I gained a whole new understanding of their personalities and the era in which they lived. I hope to offer my children and grandchildren glimpses of my life while I am still living. My grandparents and parents are very much alive in my heart today; I only wish I hadn't waited to truly know them. The courage it took for them to live their lives inspires me to live my own more honestly and wholeheartedly. It is why I want to offer stories of my life to my children and grandchildren while there is time to solidify our bond.

My parents were children during the Great Depression and bore scars from the traumas they suffered. They each lost a parent to cancer when they were young, and both needed to help care for their families in ways that left little time to be children. I did not fully understand this until later in my life when I began working in the arenas of trauma and abuse. Also, they were young adults during World War II, and that, of course, brought even more trauma into their lives. The common thinking of their generation was to just get on with life and not talk about the painful parts.

I loved my mother, but she was never a safe person. She was an impatient woman who belittled and yelled at my sister and brother and me. She was like a perfectionistic Martha Stewart, but with an unstable psyche. There were consequences to inconveniencing her, so I learned to stay out of her way and be as invisible as possible. When I developed asthma as a ten-year-old and could not breathe, it seemed safer to gasp for air and pass out on my bedroom floor than to cry out for help. I was that committed to not bothering her. Life felt much safer that way.

When I became a mom, I was infatuated with my own babies. It was an immense privilege to give birth to two daughters and a son. I was happily married, but having babies of my own was unlike any love I ever could have imagined. I didn't know it at the time, but I was being given the opportunity to reparent my own heart as I delighted in their beautiful faces. I cheered them on as they progressed through each stage of development and pondered the joy around me at those times.

Now I'm a grandmother of two stunning girls and three glorious boys. I not only get to play with them and delight in their innocence and imagination, but I also get to watch their remarkable parents delight in their children. My grandchildren fiercely love me, and I them. But to be truthful, I sometimes want to hide from those I love.

When I was a child, playing in a closet felt like a safe place to be when my mother was present. I never knew what might cause her to become angry. I've always longed for her approval, but it wasn't till her funeral that I heard she was proud of me. Many younger parts of me still long to hear her say, "Becky, you are precious to me, and I love you." I think I have been on a quest ever since I was a little girl to find out who I am in my own eyes, if not my mother's. I have been an overly cautious woman who has been more comfortable living in the shadows.

I now want to connect with others in ways I yearned to as a child. I am excited to discover the hidden gifts inside me that illuminate the path I am meant to walk in my lifetime. I feel like the time is now.

As invisible as I was to my mother, she was hidden from me as well. I have come to believe that each of us is full of treasure, just like that old wooden box that so delights my grandchildren. It is our choice whether or not to share that treasure with others. I never got to see what was inside my mother while she was living, but I will let my children and grandchildren see what is inside of me. I will risk vulnerability with my husband and my friends so that together we can enjoy the riches we have to offer one another. I will pour out on the page what I have learned about my identity, what I am still learning about intimacy, and how I am living out my calling. Maybe someday my grandchildren's children will find me hidden in plain sight and come to know the woman I have fought hard to be. I hope they will find treasures that enrich them on their own journeys and hear the echo of my voice in their hearts, saying, "You are precious to me, and I love you."

An Odd Journey

Twenty years ago today, our family moved to Bainbridge Island, Washington. The journey of founding the Seattle School of Theology and Psychology has been filled with ups and downs and twists and turns that Dan and I could not have foreseen. When my husband is asked if he would go back and do it again, he quickly says no every time.

The life we once led in Colorado seems like another lifetime ago. Since college, I had longed to live there. It was so exciting when Dan got a teaching job in Denver! Our children were old enough for hiking, skiing, and mountain biking, and we were in the prime of our lives without realizing it.

When Dan and I traveled from Indiana to Colorado to look for a house, we found an amazing planned community with a home in our price range. After signing the papers and taking photos of every room, we walked out to our new street, and Dan said, "Let's knock on that neighbor's door and see if they have children."

When a woman about our age answered the door, Dan said, "Hi! We're your new neighbors." Without hesitation she invited us in to meet her children, who were a bit older than ours, but we hoped their youngest and our middle child would be friends. We couldn't have been more excited about what lay ahead.

Colorado living was more than we had hoped for. The sun shone more than three hundred days a year, and the blizzards that swept through the state between September and June were stunning to watch, dumping feet of snow that quickly melted in the sun's warmth. We enjoyed spontaneous neighborhood dinners and celebrations as each new neighbor arrived. We had so much in common with families doing the same things we were: landscaping, volunteering at our new neighborhood school, and being part of the neighborhood book club. The swim and racket club was a few blocks away, and our kids rode their bikes to swim lessons and tennis tournaments. I never tired of the drama of blizzards and being snowed in. I loved sledding across the street, shoveling snow, and using a snowblower. The rugged beauty of Colorado was the geography of my heart, and I loved it there.

A year after we moved into our home, a new road was built in our development. At the end of the cul-de-sac was a center lot with a view of the red rocks in the valley behind the Dakota Hogback. We could even see part of Pikes Peak down the valley! I called the real-estate developer daily for more than eighteen months to see if the lot was available for purchase. One day he called to tell me, "The lot is available, and you have forty-eight hours to decide before I make it available to someone else." The economy was at a standstill at the time, but our hearts were wedded to that plot of land, and we decided to buy it.

We found an architect and a contractor and began the process of building our dream house.

Our dream home in Colorado

Better said, I had a husband who said he was too busy to have anything to do with it, and I would have to be in charge of everything! The builder and architect knew nothing about designing the Williamsburg-style home I wanted, and they laughed about it, along with the foreman, calling it a "Cape Cod dude ranch." The alternative plans they came up with were horrific to me, but my voice wasn't strong enough to faithfully stand up for what I envisioned.

When I showed the plans to my neighbor, she said, "Get on the phone and have them halt the plans because they aren't listening to you!" She knocked some sense into me, and I called the team to say that we needed to meet. Dan was furious at me for throwing a wrench into the plans that were already well underway, and I was furious at myself for letting things proceed as they had.

The meeting with the architect, contractor, and foreman was tense, to say the least. My husband could barely look at me. I had never had to stare down four angry men to make the point that they had not been listening to me. But they were listening now as I told them again what I wanted, this time in a strong voice. To this day, that was one of the hardest things I have ever had to do. To my relief, they finally heard me, and a pleasing set of house plans was eventually drawn up.

The morning we moved one street over into our new home, twenty of Dan's students came to help out. Everything felt perfect, and the house exceeded our expectations. It was an amazing gift of a lifetime. But seven years later, Dan's job in Denver came to an end, and we had to move again. I remember the day I pounded a "For Sale by Owner" sign into the front yard. I cried often as the move loomed.

When we finally left our dream home and our beloved Colorado life behind, our family made the journey to Washington State in a van, a car, and a U-Haul truck. It was the longest drive down the most driven street of my life. I led the caravan and recall the agony when more than twenty-five neighbors poured into the street for one last good-bye. At the corner I had to stop the van and let out a loud wail of sorrow. It frightened me and everyone else! My husband drove the U-Haul truck filled with his books; our son, Andrew, and Maggie, our Australian terrier, sat next to him.

When our neighbors came out to say good-bye, Maggie tried to jump out the window. The truck swerved, and Dan almost hit another car. Andrew waved good-bye to his two best friends in the whole wide world, tears streaming down his cheeks. Annie, our oldest, drove behind us in her car, needing to be alone on the long trip ahead, and Amanda was with me in the van, pressing her feet against the window, her heart as heavy and sad as mine. Isolated in our grief, we made our way to Puget Sound, listening to the same R.E.M. CD for two days.

When we finally drove off the ferry onto Bainbridge Island, my heart ached, and I couldn't help wondering, *What are we doing here? Did we make the right decision?* When the moving van arrived at our new home, we discovered that the turns in the street were too tight to maneuver it into our driveway. So we borrowed a neighbor's smaller truck and shuttled our belongings to the house, which was almost half the size of our Colorado dream home. Our garage was filled for months with things we couldn't fit into the space. Over time, however, we settled in, and I was able to meet my sorrow with grace and be grateful for the bounty of God's kindness in the midst of uprooting my heart and home.

Today it is March in the Pacific Northwest. As I look around my home and out my window, the scene is oh so different from when we first arrived.

First ferry ride to Bainbridge Island, WA

The property that was once barren is now filled with many trees and plantings that nourish our hearts. The heather is blooming and breathtaking. Our gardens are erupting, worms squirming on the patio, and the birds are being blown about in the spring wind. The marine air that sweeps in off the water and shrouds the sun for hours is not the problem it used to be. The barking sea lions in the sound no longer seem as loud as I weed and water the flowers. Gatherings of witch hazel, flowering cherry, and crab-apple branches fill the rooms in our home. Bouquets of primroses and daffodils grace counters and tabletops. This is one season when you won't hear me complain about the rain! New life and hope abound in anticipation of all the bounty that is coming with summer.

My yoga teacher once said that it's okay to set off in a direction without knowing what we will find at our destination. It's true that we don't know what the future will be like, yet we're to be faithful in moving forward, even when we question the road's "rightness" the way I did when we left Colorado. The anniversary of our move reminds me that life doesn't always offer stories that feel safe. The rootedness of our lives in this state we've called home for twenty years is strong and sweet, but I may not always live in this home or in this part of the country. Who knows where the next leg of my journey might take me? But my hope is not in avoiding tumult and loss; rather, it is in anticipating the spring that will always come again.

Today the aroma and colors of our gardens thrill my eyes and senses. God is at play. No matter where life takes me next, it feels easy now to bless this odd journey.

QUESTIONS TO PONDER

Listen for echoes of your story in this essay and write about it in your journal. Then ponder the following questions and record your thoughts.

1. Write a personal story of a hope realized that still surprises you years later.
2. What are you willing to sacrifice to see your dreams come true?
3. In what ways have you suffered to make a dream become reality?

Taking My Place

D an and I arrived late for a fund-raising dinner at the Ritz-
Carlton ballroom in Naples, Florida. We were disheveled
after a day of travel from Seattle, and it felt strange to be in a silk
summer dress in November when shortly before, I had been wearing jeans, a sweater, and boots. Our name tags instructed us to sit
at table number 8, and when we got there, two women greeted us
and said they felt like they knew me.

"It's nice to meet you, too, Dan," they added, "but we really like
your wife's writing."

This greeting was completely unexpected, and Dan laughed as he
delighted in this new chapter of our lives.

I've traveled with my husband for four decades and have usually been the invisible spouse who loves what he teaches but is
often unnoticed. I perfected this black-op art of invisibility from
an early age. My parents were part of "the greatest generation,"
Tom Brokaw's coined phrase for those who survived the Great
Depression and World War II.

Becky in her parents' arms Columbus, Ohio

With youthful exuberance, my parents gave their time to countless groups, helping orphaned boys, raising money for college scholarships for girls, funding a new wing at the art museum, building a church, and so on. I was to be a good girl, proof of their hard work and excellent character. I was never to dispute or contradict their opinions or desires. I was to be seen and not heard. Keeping quiet and out of sight was a safe haven and a wise choice at the time. And being the middle child allowed me to hone this skill even more.

Inevitably I brought those skills into my marriage and allowed Dan to navigate the conversations in our lives. Further, I married a man whose presence is large and fills a room even when he is quiet.

When I attended his conferences or whenever he preached, there was little curiosity about me, and usually I was okay with that, since I didn't feel invisible at home.

Earlier in our marriage, I rarely traveled with Dan because my life was filled with having babies, raising children, and holding down the fort. But after the nest was empty, new troubles began, and our even-keeled marriage became choppy in uncharted waters. My quietness felt like a deficiency, and I had a low opinion of myself compared to gregarious people. I felt embarrassed for not having a command of language the way talkative people did and not being able to engage others as easily as my husband did. I felt envious not only of Dan's skillful teaching but also of those who pursued him and benefited from his counseling. I became critical of his words, even nitpicking the accuracy of dates and details in the stories he told about our lives and family. I knew it was my issue to sort out, but I didn't know how to relieve the pain of feeling left out. My vision narrowed, and I began to see life through a lens of what others had and I didn't.

Then I entered a season of inquiry and a quest for identity. Who was I to be in this third phase of our marriage? My desires tossed me up and down, and I felt mean and misunderstood. The way wasn't clear, and the new terrain seemed a bit like Alice's Wonderland. Sometimes I was too big and noisy, and other times my smallness was a haven of peace or a prison of despair. It felt as if I was spinning in a dangerous dance when I happened upon the theological idea of *perichoresis*. In Greek, *perichoresis* means "rotation or dance," and in early church theology, it became a way to talk about the interplay of the members of the Trinity. The Trinity dances together in a holy mutual indwelling without a loss of identity. I love to imagine each person of the Trinity—the Father, the Son, and the Holy Spirit—voluntarily circling the other two and dancing with joy and love for one another.

I realized that the concept of *perichoresis* applies to me, too, because I have been resurrected with Christ, and there is a mutual indwelling without a loss of personal identity. Because of Jesus, I am unified with the Father and the Holy Spirit, and all that I do (play, work, create) and all that I am (a woman, wife, mother, friend, daughter) become my arena for participating in the Trinitarian life of God. Tell me this isn't wild!

I cannot dance with my husband to the sweet song of the Trinity unless I rise up and join him on the floor. I have to bring myself to him and allow him to move with me, fully independent yet intertwined, unique as an individual and yet one with him. If I fail to step onto the dance floor, or if I merely mirror my husband's moves, I won't be sufficiently distinct to offer him the fullness of who I am. Nor will I be able to join the wild dance of God's kingdom.

I see now that my quietness is as important in its own way as my husband's gregariousness in terms of connecting meaningfully with others. I have skill in listening that is being used to shine healing light on the paths of those in my care. I have grown a heart of mercy and defiance against injustice and pretense. I often notice the hurting and outcast, the lonely and the bullied. I often become a friend to odd people. There are very few people I dislike. I have come to appreciate my quietness for the good things it has given me: the ability to see, listen to, and care about people. I am acutely aware of the need people have to speak and share their souls.

I am less judgmental now of people who seem to need more attention than others. Through my own work in counseling, I've been able to forgive my parents. Acknowledging their harmful behaviors did not lessen my love for them; in fact, I think I love my parents more today than ever before. And I've come to value the strength God developed within me at a young age to stand up to bullying and injustice. This healing has allowed me to fight for causes much larger than the boundaries of my yard. My wholeness in Jesus and my appreciation of the Father's unique design in me has made my quietness seem not so deficient after all. I now embrace it for service to the kingdom.

At our dear friends' Nate and Abby's wedding last fall, Dan and I threw ourselves into the percussive movement of music with people decades younger than us. We danced until our bodies screamed, "Take me home!" Sweaty, exhausted, and alive, we held hands while we walked toward our car to the sounds of celebration.

May we all join the celebration of love and joy and dance with every move that is uniquely ours. There is no shame in being ourselves. We are meant to take our place in God's kingdom, where the King invites each of us to dance joyfully with Him and others.

QUESTIONS TO PONDER

Listen for echoes of your story in this essay and write about it in your journal. Then ponder the following questions and record your thoughts.

1. Write about a time in your life when you struggled to take your place in God's kingdom.
2. How do you feel and react when others fail to notice you?
3. When are you most apt to dance with abandon?

Child's Pose

It was another New Year's Eve, and my husband and I were eager to get into bed before nine o'clock. For a third year in a row, we were ill. It seems our bodies aren't suited to international travel in winter and the rigor of long flights. The good news: We made it through Christmas before we felt our throats and lungs betray us.

I rejoiced in knowing I didn't have to go anywhere, and I tried to be a good sport about being sick. I was a model patient, sleeping eleven hours at night, eating healthy foods, and taking homeopathic remedies. Even then, it took patience to be nice to myself (and to my husband) as I waited patiently to heal. When I'm sick, it's easy for me to condemn my weak immune system and blame myself for being less than my best. These thoughts are so sneaky, and being good to myself gives way to self-loathing and fear. "I'm going to feel like this forever! Hurry up, old body, and get well!"

Lo and behold, a morning finally came when I was well enough to leave the exile of home and go to my yoga class. I unrolled my mat in the ninety-five-degree studio, put my head down, and waited in Child's Pose, grateful to be back. But as I basked in the warmth with my eyes closed and smelled the peppermint and tea-tree oil on my mat, these thoughts came: *Am I going to be able to make it to the end of class? I probably shouldn't have come. I know I won't be able to do the balance poses well. This is going to be too hard.*

When I attend yoga class, I'm usually determined to work hard even if my heart and body are saying, "Rest." All too often I push myself like an Egyptian taskmaster lashing a Hebrew slave.

Our teacher greeted us with joy and kindness, and we sat quietly breathing as she explained the concept of *ahimsa*, which means "to not harm" in Hindi. No harm to others or oneself. Oh my, I realized in an instant that my thoughts on the mat were harmful to myself. I was doubting and fearful and judgmental.

I wonder how many times I have reaped the consequences of not listening compassionately to my body and not being kind to my heart. For example, when I developed asthma in sixth grade, I was prescribed a medication classified as a stimulant and was instructed to take one tablet each night before bed. Needless to say, over the next fifteen years, I had terrible insomnia. And I was vicious toward my body for depriving me of sleep. It was only a few years ago that I felt compassion for that young Becky who always lay in bed wide awake while everyone else slept—her family, her slumber-party friends, her ski-trip buddies. It makes me sad now to think about the mean things I would say to myself because I was unable to sleep like a normal person.

In the same way, I have been harsh with myself in my quest for acceptance. I spend too much energy wondering how others perceive me. I like to be liked, and I've lived much of my life seeking approval and trying to keep others happy with me. I remember creating a calligraphy poster for my father in art class in high school that said, "If it is possible, as far as it depends on you, live at peace with everyone" (Romans 12:18). I think that in some ways, misinterpreting that verse has enslaved to the desires of others. I know how to walk the middle, and with stealth-like determination, I often become a spineless person who is not true to myself as I strive to be all things to all people. Unfortunately, even in becoming aware of a shortcoming, I am apt to create more self-judgment.

While sitting in yoga class hearing about *ahimsa*, I was again being mean to myself. A subtle shift in my self-talk to *Oh, if I'm tired I can always rest in Child's Pose* would have changed everything. I see people around me do this often, and I feel nothing but kindness toward them. I need to be kinder to myself. This was not news to me that day, but there I was again being my own worst enemy.

In the years since flogging myself in that class, I have become better at embracing so much of me that I once loathed. I am seeing the good-heartedness that has directed my life instead of only my faults. This has been a sweet and liberating time of reconciliation with my young self and my adult self today. One of my favorite verses in the Bible is Philippians 4:8. "Finally, brothers and sisters," the apostle Paul wrote, "whatever is true, whatever is noble, whatever is right, whatever is pure, whatever is lovely, whatever is admirable— if anything is excellent or praiseworthy—think about such things." Practicing *ahisma* in the way I think about and treat myself is simply the other side of a commitment to the Hebrew concept of *shalom*, meaning "peace, harmony, wholeness, and tranquility."

Of course I will fail as I try to live out *shalom*, but this doesn't lessen my Father's delight in me. He sings over me. He never forsakes me. He calls me His beloved. He has plans to prosper me. He tells me to trust that He will always be with me. I see this trust in my grandchildren. They trust their parents and expect good things, good food, good-heartedness from them. And when they are hurt, they go to their parents and receive hugs and kindness. Simple. I need to keep my path forward simple. I think it's about time. If not now, at sixty-five, when?

In the next verse Paul wrote, "Whatever you have learned or received or heard from me, or seen in me—put it into practice. And the God of peace will be with you" (verse 9). My prayer is that I will learn to always run to my heavenly Parent when I'm hurt or feel bad. Nothing can separate me from Him. Nothing. May I practice the *ahisma* and *shalom* He embodies so I can receive His kindness.

QUESTIONS TO PONDER

Listen for echoes of your story in this essay and write about it in your journal. Then ponder the following questions and record your thoughts.

1. Tell the story of a time when you failed to listen to your body. What consequences did you experience?
2. To what extent does the pressure to perform play a part when you fail to listen to your body?
3. Name one way you can "do no harm" by being kind to yourself.

Remothering the Heart

M y mother's mother was a flighty woman and not quite grounded in reality. She never seemed to get things done on time, except for attending church. It is, at times, agonizing to tell the truth about one's family. If I were to inch closer to the truth, I would say that my grandmother was off her rocker. If I were to choose more accurate words, I'd say she suffered from some undiagnosed mental illness. I can only imagine the hardship this was for my mother, who became an adult way before she had the opportunity to be a child. No wonder she didn't know how to let me be a child either.

My parents met and married during World War II and settled in Columbus, Ohio. Part of the Civic Generation that became famous for community involvement after the war, they immersed themselves in church activities and various civic organizations.

Many of my mother's friends would recount how competent she was as a homemaker, and her peers greatly admired her cooking, housekeeping, and volunteering. I wanted to let them know the price our family paid for my mother to maintain such a reputation, but I never did. Instead, I absorbed her perfectionistic ways without knowing it.

Becky and sister Judy in Easter dresses with mother

My mother climbed the social ladder as quickly as she could. In the 1950s, the surgeons' and lawyers' wives wielded social power, but she joined right in regardless of being married to a stockbroker. As a three-year-old, I accompanied her to philanthropic meetings at all hours of the day. I knew to be silent in the car and was content to wander in the hostesses' yards during the meetings. At home I played quietly in my closet or outside so I wouldn't bother my mother, who had so much work to do … all the way to her grave.

Our home was never a place of rest, and she never ran out of chores for us to do. If there was an armchair cover on the floor and I hadn't picked it up, she would rage at me. If she came home from grocery shopping and we weren't standing on the patio to help unload, she would blow the car horn until someone came running. Before company arrived, we would all be expected to scramble to make sure that not a single item was out of place. If I forgot to rinse off my dishes and put them in the dishwasher, she would holler, "Dumb, dumb, Dora!" If I got in her way or didn't run fast enough to the car when we were leaving for school, she would shout at me until I scurried at her command. My mother expected me to strive hard to make life work, just as she had done.

This morning I had breakfast with my daughter-in-law and granddaughter and found myself dumbfounded at their interchange. Two beautiful plates were set before each of them: lovely scrambled eggs, bacon, and toast with cherry preserves. My daughter-in-law, Elizabeth, called to see if friends could go to the park with them after school today. When she sat down and told Elsa that the friends couldn't meet them, my granddaughter refused to eat and actually got up off her chair and starting hitting her mother on the back!

Elizabeth calmly replied, "I can see how that would be upsetting to you, and I understand that you're frustrated. Would you like some raspberries instead of your breakfast?"

I've learned to try to keep my mouth shut at such moments (not always successfully). Even though I have great love for my granddaughter, I would never have responded as Elizabeth did. I found myself thinking, *I wonder what it would have been like if my mother had parented that way?* I would have loved to hear my mother say to me, "I can understand how frustrated this must feel…" But strict obedience was required in my home, and my emotions were often squashed. All these years later, it's still new to me when someone gives me permission to have an emotion!

As I place my young self in Elsa's exuberant life, I can only grieve for the equally beautiful three-year-old Becky who would have been a radically different child and woman if my mother had been more like my daughters or my daughter-in-law.

Becky and her younger brother Tom and their parents

When I observe the blessings my grandchildren receive daily from their mothers and allow myself to grieve the lack of blessing in my own life, I'm able to look at my mother's driven, confused, trauma-filled life and long for her to know how much I ache for her now. I wish she had known more care and love and security and acceptance and delight in her life. How I wish that my mother could have been loved as a young child in better ways and circumstances than she was.

I have found that the kinder I learn to be to the young Becky now, the more I can grieve for the mother who had no idea how to let her be a little girl. And as odd as it may sound, the kinder I am to my mother who failed, the more I can allow my daughters and daughter-in-law to remother my heart through the care of their children. I only wish my mother and grandmother could have allowed me to do the same for them.

QUESTIONS TO PONDER

Listen for echoes of your story in this essay and write about it in your journal. Then ponder the following questions and record your thoughts.

1. Write about an experience that made you feel young and well cared for.
2. What are some of the known-but-not-told stories of your family?
3. Have there been times in your life when you needed someone else's permission to feel? Write about it in your journal.

Dreams of Paradise

The sun was soon to rise, and I was groggy from the previous day's travel. I crept past my snoring mother-in-law and opened the sliding door to step out onto the hotel's high-rise lanai in the Waikiki city jungle. For the past nine days, Dan's mother had been miserable with every activity we did. Her only happy moment was when a man in the Marriot laundry facility spoke to her. In her mind, he was flirting with her. Being kind to her took the concentration of a tightrope walker over Niagara Falls, and I would have fallen to my death a thousand times had I actually been on a tightrope.

Filled with guilt and disappointment, I called my dad, knowing he would answer the phone.

"Dad, hi, I wish you were here and not Dan's mom. I wanted you and mom to come with us but knew that wouldn't be possible. Dad, the sun is beginning to rise. I miss you."

I can remember his meditative pause as I heard him say in a nostalgic voice, "Yes, we had good times in Hawaii."

I reminisced with him about the trip we took in 1966. That long ago Christmas vacation was brought back to life over and over in my parents' home. Hawaiian albums playing on the stereo's indoor and outdoor speakers, monkey-pod bowls, straw hats, countless classic flowered shirts and dresses, and mai tais took them back to golden sunshine and good times. That trip was seared deep in my heart as family joy in paradise. It was magical thinking for a fourteen-year-old daughter who wanted her parents to be happy, and I clung ferociously to it.

Not long after returning from that trip with Dan and his mother, my father spent his final nineteen days in a hospice care facility refusing food and water. Thirteen months later, we buried my mother on Mother's Day. After her funeral we went to my parents' home, and my sister and brother and I decided to get out the Da-Lite screen and slide projector and view old family slides. I hadn't done that since high school.

In the surreal aftermath of an unexpected funeral, I unashamedly indulged my heart in viewing the youthfulness of my parents who were now gone. I sat mesmerized on a couch I had sat on hundreds of days and holidays gone by. When we got to the carousel of our Hawaii trip, I was incredulous when I saw my dull and petulant expressions.

"What was wrong with me?" I asked aloud. "Why do I look so unhappy?"

My sister answered fiercely, "Don't you remember how Mom and Dad fought the entire trip? They were miserable and couldn't get along for an hour without arguing."

I couldn't speak because that isn't at all what I remembered and had clung to for all these years. In a few sentences, my illusion of a happy family having good times in Hawaii was shattered.

As children it's easy to fit reality and illusions together like a jigsaw puzzle to keep the pictures of our pasts intact. Too often the loss of illusions simply turns our hearts hard. But while illusions need to die, dreams can be resurrected from the ashes of disillusionment. Now, fifty years after that family vacation in paradise, so many of my dreams have come true.

Five years ago, Dan and I were vacationing with friends in Hawaii. While walking on a secluded beach known mostly to locals, I imagined taking our family to Hawaii the following Christmas. Every time Dan and I went to Hawaii, I told him I wanted all of our kids to come. Every time I also told him how I longed to bring my parents here one last time. But the years got away too quickly, and plans were never made. During this vacation with friends, I think Dan finally heard me—and I heard myself.

After we returned home, we budgeted, scrimped, and saved. We used frequent-flyer miles, and I did the very thing I never do: I arranged a vacation for our entire family.

A taste of paradise in Hawaii

I found a house to rent and booked flights for eleven of us. It had been a good but, at times, hard year for all of us. Yet in the midst of our struggles, every time we got together or talked on the phone, someone would say, "I can't wait until Hawaii!"

It's easy to ruin a trip when we expect too much out of it. It is equally easy to diminish the importance of an experience because we fear being disillusioned. I hadn't expected the anticipation of our

Hawaiian vacation to be so great, and I worried that relational tensions, travel frustrations, or renting the wrong house might darken our time together. They almost did, but in the end, they didn't.

There was a dengue-fever scare on the Big Island, and this was especially troubling for Amanda and Jeff with their six-week-old daughter. But with six Amazon Prime shipments of mosquito repellent, patches, and wristbands, along with countless citronella candles and incense sticks, we all made it to the airport.

The first night of our trip, around three in the morning, Dan had horrible stomach pains. He spent hours Googling his symptoms and was convinced that he had appendicitis. Oh, Lord, he always seems to get sick! Then he found out how bad the hospital was on the Big Island, so he and I packed our suitcases to fly to Honolulu! As I carried them to the car, I told him we should first seek the advice of Amanda, who is a nurse practitioner. So at four in the morning, I knocked on Amanda and Jeff's door and asked if she could examine her dad before we left for the hospital on Oahu.

Amanda handed me sweet, swaddled Grace so she could palpate Dan's stomach. Moments later, she concluded that it wasn't his appendix, but it might be gas! In the end, we decided not to go to Oahu, but Dan didn't sleep at all that night, and things didn't get any better. Around 7:00 a.m., I tried to find out if there was an urgent-care facility nearby. Our other daughter, who is an acupuncturist, came over with her needles and helped alleviate Dan's pain. He still wanted to go to urgent care, however, so our whole family decided to go with us. It was so kind of them not to send us off alone.

In spite of Dan's health scare and various other problems, nothing dampened our family's time together. We laughed and delighted in one another. Dan and I took daily walks, praying for each family member and for the goodness of our time together. On one of the walks, we went farther than we had ever gone and ended up in an area that looked like the African savannah.

As we hiked along a trail high above the beach, we saw the outline of a large multilevel building ahead. I recognized it: the Mauna Kea resort, where my dad drove our family in a rental station wagon in 1966. It was the most expensive hotel in the world at the time. He had even asked for valet parking. When the valet opened mom's door, she got out of the car looking regal, like Audrey Hepburn. We weren't actually staying at the hotel, but my father scammed to get us onto their private beach. Dressed in our beach cover-ups, we marched through the lobby and down the grand stairway to paradise. I cringed at being imposters, but we didn't get caught. Even if my sister was right, and much of our time together was fraught with my parents' conflicts and my pouting, I remember that excursion as the most idyllic afternoon of our trip.

What if eternity is the consummation of all the dreams that have only partially come to be, not to mention the dreams we never knew we had? Do we dare to believe that in heaven suffering will not only end but be redeemed? It is too beautiful to comprehend. Yet it isn't an illusion. I believe that our final destination will be even better than we imagine—a paradise beyond our wildest dreams.

QUESTIONS TO PONDER

Listen for echoes of your story in this essay and write about it in your journal. Then ponder the following questions and record your thoughts.

1. Have you ever revised your story to make it more endurable? What revisions did you make? What did you find unendurable about the truth?

2. Describe a moment when an illusion you had was stripped away and a deeper desire was revealed.

3. Transforming grace is always surprising. Do you embrace surprises? Why or why not?

Forgiveness

It all came about quickly and unexpectedly. First, one of our children, then another, and finally the last called and said, "I'm coming over to spend the night!" Dan and I couldn't remember the last time our family had been together without their spouses and children. Our hearts were bursting with anticipation at what was about to happen.

Annie and Amanda had requested pedicures, so after Andrew picked them up on the 2:05 ferry, he dropped them off at a local salon, where I was waiting next to two seats and tubs of bubbling, soapy blue water. Following our pedicures, we stopped by the farm store and bakery because eating at home sounded better than eating out. We just had to go bask in the sunshine on our patio; we just had to be "home."

After preparing our late-afternoon snack, we lingered outside and savored each bite. It seemed like Holy Communion as we took in sustenance and looked at one another with our Ray-Ban sunglasses on. Later we fixed dinner together, just like old times. The peace and quiet without nursing babies or rambunctious grandchildren or spouses to tend to took us back to an era we had left behind almost a decade before. We didn't need words to express how we felt about the sacredness of this time and why it was happening. Amanda, our second-born, was six months pregnant and moving to New York City in two weeks. Our lives, work, and travel schedules were complicated, and this was "our" night as a family of five, probably for the last time.

As we sat down at the old, usually overcrowded dining-room table, the spaciousness of just us felt odd. Dan prayed, and then we began eating and talking. This seemed so different from when one of the children had gone off to college. There was a heavy sense of permanence in the air with Amanda's impending move. We all felt it, but no one put words to it. I had moved away from my family when I was twenty-three years old and never returned. I knew the freedom it had given me, but I also knew how costly it had been for my parents and siblings. It would have been awful for me if my brother or sister had moved and left me behind. I couldn't *not* bless my children for moving away, but I think it's always harder on the ones who get left behind.

Dan always asks great questions. As we were finishing seconds and I was thinking it was almost time to clear the table, he put forth a zinger: "Now that you're adults, what surprises you as you look back at your upbringing?"

Suddenly what started as a sweet meal turned in a direction none of us could have predicted. There was silence for quite some time. Then one of our daughters began to describe all the fear and pressure she had felt growing up. The other two nodded in agreement, and story after story came out about how lying was necessary to avoid provoking judgment when they chose to stray from what they knew Dan and I wanted.

Annie said, "Mom, before we would get out of the car once we got to church, you would say something like, 'Remember who your dad is because people will notice if you misbehave.'"

Amanda added, "You said that the Sunday school teachers knew that our dad was a seminary professor, and if we misbehaved, it would be a bad reflection on our family."

Our son said, "We all hated Awana, Mom, and you did too. You were stressed on Sunday afternoons, and none of us were good at memorizing Bible verses. Besides, I think you and Dad dropped us off just so you could go on dates together."

Then it seemed like all hell broke loose as they described the many ways they disobeyed without our knowing it. It seemed that our rigidity and inability to listen to them compelled our children to sneak off to parties without our knowing a thing about what was really going on. Other parents weren't clueless, they claimed. Other parents were understanding and didn't make their kids lie and rebel. Other parents would listen and permit a wider range of activities, but not us. Our children seemed to delight in telling each other, and us, about the escapades of rebellion we had never known about.

Truthfully, I had to admit to myself that I, too, had done many of the same things to avoid obeying rules I had grown up with. But I hadn't planned on this raucous banter that made me feel rigid, foolish, disrespected, and angry. I hadn't anticipated a food fight, but before I knew it, I picked up my ammunition and fought back. How I wish I had learned a different way of defusing conflict. Dan is brilliant at admitting his shortcomings and validating our children's feelings. I wish I could have done that! But I immediately got defensive. I wanted to explain and justify what Dan and I had said and done while raising them. It didn't seem fair to have all our years of parenting, along with so much labor, worry, heartache, and hope, summed up so negatively at a dinner-table conversation. My defensiveness always exposes my fury, and I end up feeling stupid and ashamed. Why can't I keep my mouth shut?

I tried to stop and breathe, but unfortunately, after I had listened to all their hurt and anger, tears began rolling down my cheeks. I sat silently until I could speak without crying. Everyone is okay with my tears; having a psychologist for a husband and father has taught us that tears are good. But it's hard for me when tears expose my failure. I feel as if I have been pushed into a corner, and the only way to get out is more exposure, more shame, more fury.

In that moment I felt so alone. I pleaded in my mind: *Dan, help me!* But I was on my own. "I'm sorry," I blubbered. "I'm sorry. I wish I had known better as a mom and, of course, dear Annie, our firstborn, you bore the brunt of my needing you to be good and polite and successful academically, more than your sister and brother. I'm sorry the weight was so great."

Dan looked at me across the table as if to say, *Becky, good grief, stop! You're like a runaway train!* He, on the other hand, simply agreed with them and asked their forgiveness. He defused the food fight and their fury. I felt wounded and ashamed and exposed. Why did I get caught like this? He did the thing I wished I could have done.

One child reassured us. "For all your failures, I never doubted that you loved me." Two other heads nodded, and Dan and I experienced the inexorable mingling of both failure and forgiveness. I was glad we were no longer covered with so much splatter.

We adjourned and cleaned up; then we found places on the couches to watch a couple episodes of *Odd Mom Out*, a parody of a mom in New York City trying to get her twins into kindergarten, and the courage and shenanigans she had to pull off to do so. It felt so good to have everyone's eyes off me and on a television screen. I loved being covered up with the afghan, even on a summer evening. I felt less exposed as I stretched out on one of the couches alone. I dreaded having to get up and kiss everyone good-night.

I slept poorly and was the first to rise at four thirty the next morning. Dan joined me soon after. We admitted that we were still reeling from what our kids said to us, and we shared our sorrow over failing our children.

"Let's go for a walk," I suggested after we prayed for the mercies that are new every morning. Dan and I walked and talked about how we, too, found fault with how our parents raised us. We, too, were broken as they were, and we, too, failed. Each generation is harmed in a different way simply because we are all human. Dan and I confessed our naive thinking that because we came to Christ when we were in college and had raised gospel-believing children, we expected them to not rebel as we had during our high school and college years. We were sad to realize that our strictness had hurt them.

We walked, we prayed, and we talked some more, and then we returned home ready for each of our children to wake up and be with us. We spent the day looking through old pictures together, playing dominoes, and eating pancakes with jam. And then, all too soon, eighteen holy, never-to-be-repeated hours as a family came to an end. They had passed just like the thirty-five years of raising our children: hard, sweet, and so very quickly.

With my parents in heaven, I find that I love them more and more. I didn't know that this would happen. I didn't know that the shelf life of love doesn't expire, but in fact extends. When Dan and I first moved into our home on Bainbridge Island, I painted 1 Peter 4:8 on our kitchen wall: "Above all, love each other deeply, because love covers over a multitude of sins." It's true, and it is our only hope through failure and regret. We are a gospel-needing family whose sins are covered by Jesus's blood. We are free because of His love, and if we cannot love with joy and without resentment and forgiveness, then we are the biggest fools of all. Fortunately for Dan and me, our children have offered us forgiveness, honor, and love in spite of our failures. Love covers our sins and defuses our shame. I am so grateful.

QUESTIONS TO PONDER

Listen for echoes of your story in this essay and write about it in your journal. Then ponder the following questions and record your thoughts.

1. What personal story about forgiveness reminds you that being forgiven can be both awkward and sweet?
2. When have you had a hard time asking for forgiveness?
3. How do you respond when someone forgives you?

The Green Monster

A t various times throughout my life, a friend has said something like Margaret said more than thirty years ago. As
young moms, we called on each other for help while raising our
children far from the states where our families of origin lived. We
had similar work ethics and propensities to keep our homes in
order. Our yards were extensions of our homes. With toddlers in
tow, we even tried to keep our cars clean!

I never thought much about it, but Margaret and I were cut
from the same cloth. Our husbands were both completing their
doctorate programs while teaching at the same school. Margaret
and I understood that taking meals to sick friends and reaching
out to those whose husbands were out of work was important.
We were used to being all things to all people. We taught Sunday
school, hosted parties, and volunteered for all kinds of activities.
We took holidays seriously, baking cookies, nut breads, and cakes.
We were serious about teaching our children the Westminster
Catechism. I considered us really good friends until one day, out
of the blue, Margaret said, "I was telling someone how I felt about
you, and I had to say that as much as I like Becky, I will never be
as skinny as she is or have as much money as she has."

I felt as though I had been punched in the stomach. I didn't know how to respond. Was this a compliment? Was it a slur? All I know is that it tasted of envy, and I never felt quite at ease with Margaret again.

Envy is a killer of love and trust. It is a kiss of death between friends, or even acquaintances. I have had my fair share of envy with friends who have had more money, more children, more prestige, bigger houses, more beauty, more talent, and so on. It can be a severe practice to get that vice under control. If I'm unable to, I had better just end the friendship, because it will only suffer under the lash of the Green Monster.

I remember when I struggled with getting pregnant and staying pregnant. In the depths of my despair, I had a hard time being friends with women who had more children than I had. It was childish of me to be so sensitive, but my longing for another baby was like a chokehold. I never told anyone how envious I felt and had to be careful not to expose my sorrow by counting babies.

I suffered my first miscarriage before leaving the house to teach kindergarten on a Friday morning. I felt that my job would be in jeopardy if I told anyone that I was hoping to start a family. I just called in sick that day and told no one. It never occurred to Dan or me that grieving a miscarriage was legitimate. We told only one couple, and the husband said to Dan, "Be nice to Becky." That was our only counsel.

The second miscarriage was much more devastating after almost two years of trying to get pregnant. Because of our move to a new state, we met our doctor for the first time at the emergency room. I stayed in the hospital for a day, and when "viability" was finally ruled out, I had a D and C. I remember a couple of days later going to watch Dan play tennis with one of his classmates in his doctoral program.

When I described to her how I was doing, she said, "Becky, you're grieving." I was shocked that such a thing was allowed. I had actually felt deficient because I was so sad.

The third miscarriage happened in yet another city that was new to us. I never thought of calling Dan at his new teaching job and asking him to come home when my fears were realized. I miscarried alone a few days after my mother and sister had taken Annie to Ohio so I could rest in bed to protect our unborn child.

Becky and Annie

Once again, I hadn't had a chance to meet my new doctor before miscarrying, and since I didn't want to inconvenience Dan, I called a student's wife, whom I had never met, and asked her to drive me an hour away to meet my obstetrician in the neighboring rural town.

I numbly filled out a form and handed it to the receptionist. I was still spotting and went to the bathroom before going to the examination room. A lovely cross-stitched sampler on the wall next to the sink read "Don't worry! You won't be pregnant forever." The insensitivity shocked me, but I stoically wiped away my tears.

The doctor was sympathetic when we met. Thankfully he didn't think I would need a D and C. However, right before he left the room, he said that Dan and I should wait four months before trying to get pregnant again. Four months! A third of a year! It seemed an interminable sentence to an infertile woman who had a one-in-three chance of success.

After that I cringed at being with friends who spoke in front of me about their complex feelings related to unexpected pregnancies. It was so painful to hear, yet it was also too painful to speak about how I would give anything for such a thing to happen to me. My sadness was so great that I even refused to tell people I was trying to get pregnant. The few times I did speak about my infertility, I regretted it because my broken heart was exposed and often mishandled.

Dan and I eventually had Amanda and then Andrew with the help of fertility drugs. Since then I have been around quite a few women who have miscarried. Nowadays these couples are usually cared for so beautifully. They name their babies and bury them in tiny coffins with ceremonies to honor their grief.

A friend of mine flew home early from a conference to be with her son and daughter-in-law during their miscarriage. It triggered such a sense of loss for me. I could not imagine having a mother or mother-in-law stand beside me through such grief. I never even asked my busy husband to enter and remain in my sorrow. He never thought I needed such care or understood that a miscarriage was a loss that required deep grieving. Now I'm stunned by how careless, foolish, and blind both of us were.

During those painful years when loss after loss fueled my envy of families that were growing, I had no clue how to process my feelings.

I know that most people think envy is rather easily resolved by being grateful for what we have rather than wishing for what we don't have. I agree, but not wholeheartedly. Indeed, we are to be grateful for what we have been given. But I think the anguish of envy is better addressed by fully experiencing the loss of what we desperately long for but don't have. I need to understand that my envy disguises an ache so deep that merely to dismiss it, even with gratitude, is to deny the holiness of a God-given desire.

I wonder what it would have been like to bless my desire for children without being filled with envy and begrudging others the joy of having babies when I was struggling with infertility. I wish I'd had the maturity to do that, but I needed healing first.

Dan and I recently did a podcast with dear friends Jeanette and Campbell, who have suffered immense heartache because of miscarriages and infertility. We all spoke honestly about the struggle and hard, rocky road to healing. As we shared with our audience, I realized that my old pain is still not fully resolved; the ache to have children is still there in my body, even as a grandmother. The losses are like wounds that have left permanent scar tissue. But as the four of us shared our pain, my scars didn't need to be hidden or denied. They were front and center and part of our discussion. What at one time filled my heart with envy, I was now free to offer as a story to bring comfort to others. And as I have come to bless the goodness of what my heart desires, what once induced envy now offers solace. I bless what I have; I bless what I do not. I still struggle with envy, but it isn't a monster anymore. Rather, it is a truth teller that reveals to me all that my heart desires and will one day have abundantly when I return to God's bosom and am blessed in full.

QUESTIONS TO PONDER

Listen for echoes of your story in this essay and write about it in your journal. Then ponder the following questions and record your thoughts.

1. When have you struggled with the "green monster"?
2. How was envy addressed in your family of origin?
3. How can fully embracing the anguish of an unfulfilled longing set you free from envy?

The 47th Parallel

My husband and I live in a bipolar state on the 47th parallel. It is a land of extremes. In the winter, the sun sets a little after four o'clock in the afternoon and doesn't rise until eight in the morning. When we drive on Bainbridge Island at night in the rain, it's so dark that twenty miles per hour can seem risky. We don't have to look for black ice, but we do have to watch for standing puddles that can cause us to swerve.

When we purchased our home on the island, our builder mentioned no less than thirty times that there were windows on all four sides of the house. I thought it was odd that he kept mentioning that fact. If I remembered correctly, all our homes and apartments had windows on all four sides. What was his point? Now I know. We need every shred of light we can get! In the summer, we Washingtonians become almost manic with sunshine joy! We stay up late and wake up with the sun. We make up for all the winter hibernation we have endured. We never take the sunshine for granted and greet one another for months with phrases like "Isn't this sunshine amazing?"

The significance of extremes has become deeply rooted in my body. As the years go by, I am more able to lean into rhythms of ebb and flow with the sun and the tides. I endure the darkness with vigorous exercise, aromatherapy, and sleep. I try to make allowances for the low times with an all-day date in bed with candles and a good book. In the summer I make peace with the birds that start singing at four in the morning and chuckle at the memory of my father's annoyance with those same creatures when my parents used to visit.

I haven't always been comfortable with extremes. My father's family was inundated with bipolar depression, and I was ambivalently attached to him. I adored him, but I couldn't depend on him. He often affirmed and delighted in me, but he was burdened by his own demons and depressions. His manic states caused erratic and grandiose behavior. When he was well, he was the family nurturer, and his laughter and smile were in stark contrast to my mother's strict, unsmiling, burdened, and social-climbing life. He knew how to play and she did not.

Becky and her dad

Sometimes my father was wild and fun. We would dance in crazy costumes to Rodgers and Hammerstein classics and take motorcycle rides, arriving home four hours later than planned.

My dad's odd and hilarious sense of humor reminded me of Groucho Marx, and we would memorize lines and act as if we had cigars in our hands, flicking off ashes and mimicking Groucho's walk. Once when we were vacationing at a famous resort, dressed in lovely clothes, my father left the price tag hanging from his hat. On the elevator, when someone informed him of the dangling tag, he would turn and say, "Did you not know that I am the Minnie Pearl of the Northwest?" My children and I would stifle our giggles at the startled reactions of well-mannered elevator mates.

But just as often, my dad was not well or available. He was a stockbroker, and often, in a matter of hours, a gloom would settle over our family if the Dow Jones Industrial Average plummeted. I remember when I was away at college my junior year, and the stock market plunged. My mother wrote to tell me my father was in a depression, and he was "bad." I found a ride home from Colorado to Ohio, and when I arrived, I thought my father looked one hundred years old. He sat stiffly in a chair, and his voice cracked when he tried to talk. I felt so helpless and couldn't wait to go back to school.

In the fifties, no one talked about being bipolar, but my mother often scolded me not to give in to those highs and lows. I think she was just afraid. And she caused me to be afraid too. I did have highs and lows, especially as a teenager. I think most teenagers do. But I lived much of my life trying to be the stable and solid member of our family. I learned to avoid the dreaded extremes by being suspicious and critical of any desire that raised the tide of anticipation. I wanted to try out for a play, but I talked myself out of it by focusing on my failures. I wanted to answer questions in class but feared that my answers would sound stupid if they were different from what someone else might say. I wanted to talk with a cute boy, but I chose to sit quietly in study hall and keep my head down. I poked holes in desire so that it would sink before it sank me. Even now sometimes, it feels risky and selfish to desire, ask, and choose space and time for myself. I find it much easier to support the desires of my husband and my children and grand-children. It has been safer and easier to birth their dreams than to nurture mine.

In one of my low seasons, I found a note in my purse from the mother of a friend of Andrew's. I can see it even now in my mind, scribbled on a yellow-lined scrap of paper. On it was an address where Moms In Prayer International, a mothers' support group, was meeting. I knew I was sinking, and this was where I needed to go. I drove to the address and was met with kindness. I wasn't sure at first if they were my type of people, but I knew I needed to be grounded in Scripture.

During the meeting I felt like I said things I shouldn't have, but I was compelled to return the following week. I began to pray weekly with women who knew Jesus and spoke the language of love. Their prayers for each other's children were pure. There was no competi-tion among them, only prayers of goodness on behalf of each child and family. As I began to let my guard down and ask for prayer for my family and myself, I realized I had unjustly confined myself in a prison of my own making.

I now know that much of my insecurity and self-loathing came from parents who had much trauma in their lives. They were un-able to bless and encourage and delight in me consistently, the way my soul longed for. I internalized their moods and found little joy in who I was. As I have learned to embrace the extremes on the 47th parallel, I have become less fearful of not being stable and even keeled. I resist the dark less and love the light more. I am aware of how short life is for me now. I see my heavenly Father wink at me and say, "You are mine, and I delight in you! Get over yourself and live with more joy!"

Today I am blessing desire, dreaming, and taking up space and time for myself. I'm learning to be kinder to myself. Jesus assures me that my ups and downs are not so dangerous; they just make me like everyone else. He is helping me set aside my critical inward gaze and see myself as He does.

QUESTIONS TO PONDER

Listen for echoes of your story in this essay and write about it in your journal. Then ponder the following questions and record your thoughts.

1. Do you personally know someone who struggles with a mental illness—a family member, friend, neighbor, coworker, or even yourself? How has it affected your life?
2. What extremes do you fear or tend to avoid?
3. How has family trauma leaked into your life?

Zone 5

When Dan and I drove up the driveway to our new Bainbridge Island home in 1998, the grass was knee high. Our builder had told me he would have it cut before we arrived. I guess he had more important things to do. We came without a lawn mower because ten years earlier, my husband decided that he would rather work on Saturday mornings and hire out lawn maintenance. Now we were at our new home with a one-acre lot, and I didn't know what to do with it. So I contacted our builder for landscaping recommendations.

The Northwest is a haven for gardeners where plants are adored and doted on. I purchased my *Sunset Western Garden Book* and began the process of acclimating myself to zone 5, better known as "Marine Influence along the Northwest Coast." Entranced by the abundance of flora this climate allowed, I scheduled meetings with landscapers, anticipating flowers and fruits and vegetables galore. The midrange landscaping estimates were $50,000! I was crestfallen as I realized that if I wanted to beautify our weed-ridden property, I would have to become a self-taught amateur landscaper.

I hired a few men to help put in an irrigation system and plant some fruit trees, flowering cherry trees, and bushes and blooms to make any gardener's heart soar. I kept reading about zone 5, studying every business in town and noting what native plants they used, and became an obsessed wanderer through the local nurseries, living for the sales at the end of each season and lusting after ground covers, heathers, camellias, azaleas, lavender, and boxwood. I turned into a plant addict with dirt-stained fingers and longed to spend every moment in the yard.

Our Bainbridge Island side yard

As the years went by, however, the yard became too much for me to maintain. The lavender bushes became too leggy. The fruit trees brought all the deer and raccoons from the surrounding forest. Our raised beds were the salad bar for every four-footed creature imaginable. Plants grew so big that even though I had allowed for growth, hundreds of dollars of bushes, ground covers, and fruit trees had to be pulled out or cut down. I was easily in the yard forty hours a week weeding, fertilizing, and pruning. No one seemed to notice the beauty, and certainly no one appreciated the sacrifice of time. After fourteen years of labor, I became bitter and regretted trading tennis for plants.

I had tried to enlist my husband in planting. *I'll get him to want to be home more*, I thought. *I'll get him to be grounded. I'll get him hooked on the joy of watching our plants grow instead of complaining about the rain. I'll get him to enjoy fresh plums and English peas.* But that never happened. I felt sorry for myself with a husband who was frequently away for work and recreation. I seethed as I pulled weeds until the lovely five o'clock "adjustment hour" arrived; then I gathered all that anger into my glass of wine and drank it alone with snarly defiance. When I paid our monthly bill for the slip where our sailboat was moored, I noted with exasperation how little we sailed. As I allowed my anger to seed my heart, the joy of gardening became as soggy as the soil. The root of bitterness is a nasty weed that grows deep if not eradicated.

During this time, both of my parents died within a year of each other, and our two youngest children went away to college. Even our dog of fourteen years died. I felt so empty, sad, and lost. In this tumult of loneliness and grief, I confided in a friend my husband had trained in counseling. She was two decades younger but had keener eyes than my own. With a heart of a desperate wife, I took her counsel to face all that needed to be named. I saw that our home had become a bit like a hospital over the years. It was as if we always had people in our hallways with crutches and casts and bandages around their heads. Too many came for Dan's care, and I became so jealous, I couldn't see straight! His affection for others and his attentiveness to them became salt in the many wounds of my life. When his schedule permitted some freedom, he longed for time away where no cell phones could reach him. That wasn't what my soul longed for. I wanted roots at home, friends who were not my husband's colleagues, friends who didn't need his advice and fixing. I wanted to be first in his life. But we were at odds with each other, and I became self-righteous. I asked for what I wanted in ways that were demanding and harsh.

With the help of my friend and another acquaintance who became my coach via Skype, I was able to confess my resentment toward Dan and receive the help I needed. Slowly, slowly this work of hope in a renewed life took root. My desire for beauty deepened, and I learned to articulate what I wanted without fury. I realized that I needed to change myself rather than my husband. What began as "his" issues were so clearly mine as well. First the log out of my own eye! It was rocky, and sometimes our voices were way too loud in our yard. "Honey, not so loud," I would say, but Dan would just turn up the volume, and I wondered how much our neighbors heard. That's how change can be sometimes. Embarrassing. Frightening. Messy.

A couple of years later, the sailboat left the water and lived next to the garage for a year or two. Finally the dream of owning a boat died for my husband, and it went up for sale. I knew I would soon have money to hire some yard help. It was a bittersweet afternoon when an enthusiastic man came with cash, and the many one-hundred-dollar bills were counted on the kitchen table. As he drove down our driveway with our West Wight Potter, I watched from an upstairs window and prayed that the trailer tires wouldn't go flat. Surprisingly, I wasn't relieved or happy to know that gardening help was near. I was sad for both of us because the dream to sail had died on the vine. Some dreams just don't bloom.

But my relationship with my husband was thriving. I no longer resented him or the boat. I began traveling with the Allender Center team and hearing my husband teach about trauma and abuse. I heard many things that applied to the longings of my own heart, and I entered into two years of group work. By being on the front lines with others seeking wholeness and doing battle for one another, I was healed of trauma in ways I never could have imagined.

As Dan and I enter our Medicare years, we're equipped to serve together. The bride who watched so many others receive care and counsel from her husband is now well enough to minister alongside him. It is something I never could have foreseen as I weeded alone and drank away my anger while the sun was setting on our lovely patch of land. What joy I now possess! My hope is no longer in changing my husband. My hope is in the God of the universe who understands my needs far better than I do. Each day I see my need for Jesus in deeper ways, and I'm learning to own my part in nurturing the happiness and fulfillment I long for in our marriage.

I now have funds to pay others to weed my yard. I'm grateful for their care and for the money to pay them. But what was once a passion and important to my identity is no longer. I love my yard and the beauty it displays throughout the seasons, but few compliments come our way, and it is well with my soul. The most deadly plant, bitterness, has been seized by the hands of prayer and yanked out by its roots. Wild beauty abounds in my yard and, more important, in my heart. I am forever grateful for this new season.

QUESTIONS TO PONDER

Listen for echoes of your story in this essay and write about it in your journal. Then ponder the following questions and record your thoughts.

1. What dreams in your life need to die for deeper desires to take root and grow?
2. What dreams have died and prevented new desires from springing to life?
3. How has bitterness or envy kept you from participating in the promise of the resurrection?

Sex?

Today began in the darkness of yet another Pacific Northwest rainstorm. I walked to the front porch to plug in our Christmas lights. A month past Christmas, I thought they would help us endure the gloom of the relentless pouring rain and darkness at seven in the morning. In other states we would have been labeled "white trash" at worst or just plain odd to display Christmas lights on January 21st, but in this part of the country in an El Niño year, it's a relief to see light in any form. I actually feel like I'm helping my neighbors with our lights; sometimes I leave them on all day.

About fifteen minutes after I handed my husband his coffee with foamed milk and a smidge of cinnamon, I remembered what day it was. "Happy anniversary! I love you. Thirty-nine years ago at this time, we would have been at the bridal brunch."

We smiled as we drank our coffee and powered up our computers, moving softly into our morning routine.

Regrettably I tried to sign into iCloud. Five different passwords made that long, skinny rectangle shimmy in a defiant squiggle. "I hate this!" I harrumphed.

Becky and Dan on their wedding day

Dan said, "I can't begin another morning like we did yesterday. Give me some time to figure this out." (Yesterday, my computer passwords weren't syncing, three documents I had worked on disappeared, and my iTunes password had to be changed several times.)

It felt like the millionth time I had needed my husband to get me unstuck since I started trying to manage banking, taxes, health-care reimbursement, and writing online. I missed knowing how to do things that were once easy for me when I could do them on paper.

I went upstairs to dress for yoga, knowing that I probably wouldn't go because I had a blog to write about sex, and I couldn't even get into my computer. And not just sex, alas, but "Sex?" was the topic I'd been given. Isn't sex difficult enough to address without adding a question mark?

Welcoming the procrastination imposed by my inability to log on to my computer, I fiddled around upstairs long enough to ensure I wouldn't be going to yoga on my anniversary. We weren't even going out to dinner on our anniversary. We didn't want to. Who wants to leave the house at night in the pouring rain? I like our warm kitchen, flickering candles, a fireplace, and the beauty of Christmas lights outside our window. I like wearing pajamas for dinner!

When I came downstairs in yoga clothes with a small hope of "home practice" today, Dan was working on setting up 1Password on my computer. Oh my goodness. My love language is "quality time." I told him that this was the best anniversary gift I could think of, as I'd been hearing how this program could make my life easier.

Let's just say that within fifteen minutes, things were not going well. My husband was stymied by how Safari Outlook was not reacting the way his Gmail account had, and the mood in the room nosedived. Witnessing Dan's uncertainty about what was happening on my computer, I felt tears well up as the haunting soundtrack of *Jaws* began reverberating throughout my body.

I stood up, took a breath, and blurted out, "I hate my life"—and then quickly asked forgiveness for that outburst because I believe there is power in the spoken word. But this technical stuff was traumatizing me.

I went to the kitchen and began fixing our breakfast. When I brought our plates to the table, I said, "I love fixing eggs. I know I can succeed! I love doing laundry. I know I can succeed!" I listed other things that affirmed that I am a functional human being and made both of us laugh. In fact, we couldn't quit laughing. And the gloom and anxiety fell away.

"Dan, remember when you wanted to go sailing?" I said. "I knew twenty-eight knots of wind was too strong for our boat and our skills. I knew that, but you wanted to go, and I knew I would be miserable if you went without me. So I went, and we almost tipped over. It was the last time we ever sailed together in that boat. Still, I was so glad we were in this life together. I feel the same now with passwords mixed up and you knowing how to do things on your computer but not mine. I'm scared and I don't like it, but we can do this. We can live this life."

That is a roundabout way to explain how I feel about sex. I miss what was once so easy. Our first few years of marriage were blissfully sexual, especially on Sundays. We didn't realize the blessedness of that time before we had children. Our bodies were young and reactive, and our time was our own. After Annie was a year old, we hoped to get pregnant again. It was a five-year wait before Amanda was born, and that was a lot of sex on schedule. Add Dan's weeks away teaching seminars and his weekly commute to another state to teach, and this was a regimen of agony that caused us to lose heart about intimacy. We went through ten years of infertility and three miscarriages. I bore the weight of temperature keeping and doctors' appointments. Dan bore the burden of sex on demand. He was the sperm bank, and my womb was too often a time bomb of doom.

I miss the mystery of the first time we had sex. I miss our strong bodies and the vitality of organs in their youth. I miss the hope of conceiving during sex. I miss sex at any time of the day or night. I miss the arousal that came with the monthly cycle of being female. I miss the fun of quick, unexpected sex that sparked delight and laughter. I miss what once was and is no longer. It seems the "in sickness" part of our wedding vows is showing up all too often these days.

Dan finished his omelet, and we sat back on the couch huddled together with my computer on his lap. Each stroke of the keys brought more frustration and confusion. But he didn't quit, and I didn't panic. The touch of his thigh against mine felt arousing. His refusal to throw in the towel felt life giving.

Is this sex? Whatever it is, early in the morning or wherever it leads later in the day, I know this: I need to be open to and curious about what it means for me to be sexual until my last breath. I want to continue exploring the multifaceted experience of intimacy with my husband for the rest of our days, in sickness and in health and in spite of the sometimes maddening challenges of everyday life.

Sex? Oh yes.

QUESTIONS TO PONDER

Listen for echoes of your story in this essay and write about it in your journal. Then ponder the following questions and record your thoughts.

1. Write a story about a time when your partner's kindness and sacrifice aroused you sexually.
2. What barriers keep you from feeling sexually alive?
3. Do you give yourself permission to feel sexually aroused when your partner casually touches you? Why or why not?

Danger Ahead

It was midafternoon when the call came.

"Hi, Mom," Andrew said.

I knew instantly that something was wrong.

"I'm okay, Mom. I just went through the rear window of a woman's car, and my boss is coming to get me and take me to the hospital."

"Andrew, what happened?"

"I was making a delivery, and the woman in front of me slammed on her brakes. I didn't have time to stop. I'll be okay."

Andrew was attending college, but he put his heart and soul into being a bike messenger. He was a fixed-gear bicyclist, which meant that his bike had no gears or brakes, and the only way to stop was to fishtail the rear wheel in similar fashion to the way a skier stops while going downhill. I tried to imagine what had happened and why he hadn't called 911.

"I'll be there as soon as I can," I told him.

My heart raced, my knees felt wobbly, and there was a roaring sound in my ears. I glanced at the clock and checked the ferry schedule while grabbing a coat and a backpack. Then suddenly I stopped. Strangely enough, I decided that I was not going to rush to the 3:30 ferry after all. I needed to slow down.

I called our daughter, a nurse practitioner in Seattle, and she said that she was available to go to the ER right away.

I exhaled in relief. "Thank you, Amanda. Call me when you're with him. I will be on the 4:40 ferry."

In spite of—or because of—what I might find when I got there, prayer seemed to be the best thing for my heart before leaving the house with a wobbly body. It was an unusual, new kindness to myself to have a cup of tea and pray and center myself before rushing to the scene. I have a wise yoga teacher who says, as she has us stay in difficult poses, "Learn to pause and breathe." I am taking what I learn on the mat off the mat. More and more in my life demands that I pause and breathe. For me, that also means pausing and praying.

Prayer isn't always the first thing I do when danger intrudes. Soon after we moved to our home on Bainbridge Island, four large dogs viciously attacked our Australian twenty-pound terrier in our yard.

Our beloved Maggie

I looked out the window and saw Maggie fighting for her life. The growling and barking was horrifying, and by the time I got to her, she was in the jaws of our neighbor's German shepherd! Like any mother, my amygdala is set to protect those I love. I began screaming and kicking the dogs and eventually grabbed Maggie out from between Zeus's teeth and ran with her into our house. I hollered for Andrew, who was ten at the time, to get a towel, and we rushed to a vet's office. It wasn't until we were halfway there that I thought to pray.

Danger with a capital *D* automatically triggers our limbic system to shift into fight, flight, or freeze. But somehow, even though my body was panicked over Andrew's phone call, I knew I needed time with God to be the mom Andrew needed in the ER. Help was on the way to him; our daughter would be the first responder in the family. Meanwhile, I took time to prepare my heart and mind. This could end up being a long night.

I used to pride myself on being strong and capable of handling stress in various situations. "I can do this myself!" "No, I don't need any help." "Oh, I feel fine," even when I don't feel fine or even know how I feel. I too often reject the part of me that needs anything. As I've learned to reflect on my story, I recognize the many anxious ways I've lived within my body, and I see reasons why I developed certain survival mechanisms. Now I try to be aware of my body and my surroundings when danger presents itself and to have compassion for my anxiety.

Amanda called as I was walking off the ferry and said, "He looks worse than I thought. There is so much blood!"

What? My daughter, the nurse practitioner, was alarmed about too much blood? I could feel my heart pounding again as I arrived at the ER. Nothing prepares us for times like these, when we hang between "Please, God" and "What now?"

When I arrived at the hospital, Amanda gave me an update on Andrew before she left. Then a nurse ushered me to his room, and I saw that his forehead was glass punctured and bloody. The emergency-room physician advised us to wait until the radiologist read the X-rays.

Three hours later, the radiologist called me as he was looking at the films and said there was quite a bit of glass remaining in Andrew's forehead. I birthed this boy, and when I held him in my arms, sweet, beautiful Andrew was perfect, without blemish. Now, the radiologist explained, there was danger if his wounds weren't taken care of immediately. He advised us not to leave the hospital until a plastic surgeon could see Andrew. But the hospital staff informed us that no plastic surgeon was available at this hour, and they wanted to release Andrew.

The care from the ER doctor had been adversarial from the start, and the fact that the ER personnel had given us no hope of a plastic surgeon coming left little reason in my mind to demand a room for the night. The ER nurse wrapped Andrew's head in so much gauze that he appeared to be wearing a foot-tall, white (and red-spotted) turban.

It was almost midnight when Andrew and I left the hospital. His turban immediately started turning red from the blood oozing from his cuts, and I worried what the night might bring. Maybe I should have checked him into the hospital in spite of the staff's resistance. I didn't have a car, and I worried that the twelve city blocks to my daughter's condo might be too far to walk given Andrew's trauma. But there was no other way than walking, so walk we did, alongside gawkers who were also on the streets at midnight.

We finally made it to the lobby of the condominium, where a doorman gave us a key fob, since Annie and Driscoll were out of town. When Andrew and I entered the condo, we both found a bed, and Andrew fell asleep almost immediately. I waited up for Dan, who had been teaching at a seminar. It was wonderful to feel his care and presence when he arrived. I had carried so much of the weight of Andrew's accident alone. What a privilege it was to bear this burden with a husband who loved me wildly. What a gift that Dan was a dad who loved Andrew with all of his heart.

The next week Andrew, against his wishes, had an appointment with a plastic surgeon. He was furious and kept saying it was going to be a waste of money to keep the appointment. Being a fixed-gear bicyclist, he liked the scars on his forehead; they were like a badge of honor. We had come to a precipice of differences. The radiologist's caution about glass working its way into the brain had lodged in my gut. I decided to call Amanda, who was working nightshift, to see if she could go with Andrew to the plastic surgeon's office. She agreed, and I hoped Andrew would be less adversarial with his sister!

The surgeon had great advice about some plastic surgery and closing Andrew's ear gauges as well. Andrew held his ground and said no to both. To this day, he likes his scars and gauges, and as I age, I bless his ownership of his body more and more. I have become more aware that I am really only in charge of one body— my own. I think Andrew is still very handsome, and most people probably don't even notice his scars. I have come to peace with his ear gauges, too!

We all have stories of danger in our pasts, and we will all, unfortunately, have countless future stories of danger. Danger is written into a fallen world, and our brains are wired to engage it. But whenever possible, we are wise to slow down and choose to do so prayerfully. We are also wise to allow our loved ones to walk through danger in their own ways. Now that my kids are adults, my instruction is over unless they ask for my advice. My role now is to simply give them my blessing whenever I can. When I disapprove of a choice they make or a relationship they're in, I take it to Jesus in prayer unless my opinion is sought. (This seldom happens, and my husband and I pray together for our children more often than ever!)

I'm challenged daily to enter this world with a heart ready to face the fray, but to do so with a cup of tea and prayer. When I allow God to calm my anxious heart and body, I can arrive at the scene bearing wisdom and grace.

QUESTIONS TO PONDER

Listen for echoes of your story in this essay and write about it in your journal. Then ponder the following questions and record your thoughts.

1. Have you ever regretted how you handled a crisis? What do you wish you had done differently?
2. In a crisis, do you tend to fight, flee, or freeze? How does that look for you?
3. What would it cost to care for yourself before you care for others?

Warrior Pose

In yoga, the Warrior Pose is called *Virabhadrasana*, a Sanskrit name originating from Virabhadra, a great warrior hero in Indian mythology. The Warrior Pose is a vigorous yoga posture that demands strength and steadiness. Like many yoga poses, the Warrior requires concentration and increases body awareness. As I practiced the Warrior Pose over the years, I had no idea that my daughter's trip to Russia would send me on a warrior journey that would be far more demanding than anything I had ever done in yoga.

In the summer of 2002, Amanda went with fifteen high school classmates to Novosibirsk in southwest Siberia. They stayed in a private dacha built by a Bainbridge Island family who has a love for Russian orphans. A dacha is a seasonal or year-round home intended for the recreational getaways of city dwellers, and the one this family built was for the purpose of providing orphans who had never been out of an urban setting some time in the countryside. The family launched a program called Camp Siberia that encouraged students to raise money and volunteer their time helping Russian orphans. Amanda and the other students signed up for the program and were assigned two teenage orphans for two weeks at the dacha in Novosibirsk.

It was a life-changing experience for our daughter. She soon learned that these precious teens wouldn't have the opportunity for an ongoing education after being released from the orphanage at age seventeen. Most likely they were destined to become prostituted women. Amanda was furious to discover that many children who should have been so full of promise would instead become victims of the global sex-trafficking industry.

My husband and I were excited to meet Amanda at Sea-Tac Airport when she returned home in July. We hadn't even driven out of the airport parking lot before she said, "The girls I was with for two weeks don't get to go to college when they leave the orphanage. Did you know that?"

With fury in her voice that we hadn't heard before, our daughter quickly educated us about a world we knew little about. Prostitution and sex trafficking are the same human-rights catastrophes, she explained. Both are part of a system of gender-based domination that makes violence against women and girls profitable to a mind-boggling extreme. Both prey on women and girls vulnerable to poverty, discrimination, sexual abuse, and violence and leave them traumatized, sick, and impoverished. Both reward predators sexually and financially, strengthening the demand and criminal operations that ensure the supply. The concerted efforts of some governments and nongovernmental organizations (NGOs) to separate sex trafficking from prostitution—to treat them as distinct and unrelated phenomena—are nothing less than a deliberate political strategy aimed at legitimizing the sex industry and protecting its growth and profitability.

Amanda didn't hesitate to put her father on the spot. "Dad, you care about sexual abuse. What are you going to do about this?"

The demanding attitude of our privileged teenager set my husband off. He retorted, "I have enough on my plate with my calling to address sexual abuse. I can't handle any more."

Without skipping a beat, Amanda turned her gaze to me and said, "Mom, what are *you* going to do about this?" It was a question that seared deep into my heart and continues to haunt and propel me fifteen years later.

During Amanda's senior year of high school, my husband was asked to speak at the second global conference of the International Christian Alliance on Prostitution (ICAP). We met hundreds of people from more than thirty countries who had left good jobs to stand up to evil and say, "Not on my watch!" These people transformed my life with what they were doing to stop the violence of sex trafficking in their cities.

In addition to attending conferences and legislative gatherings on sex trafficking, Dan and I connected with people worldwide who worked in various overt and covert ways fighting for the rights of vulnerable women, men, and children. What I learned stunned me. I couldn't believe that trafficking in human beings is now one of the largest sources of income for international organized crime, netting billions of dollars each year, and that every year, thousands are forced into the commercial sex trade, exploited and abused for financial gain.[1]

Contrary to popular belief, few women and girls freely choose to become involved in the sex trade. What little girl aspires to become a prostituted woman? Various factors make women and children vulnerable to exploitation, including poverty, addiction, and abuse. Violence and pornography are often used to traumatize and desensitize women and children who are caught in prostitution and the commercial sex trade, and traumatized individuals tend to minimize their experiences, especially when they experience ongoing trauma.

For those who minister to prostituted women, it isn't about facts and figures or even mobilizing outrage and action; it's about sweet, fragile, beautiful people. It's important not to dismiss a child's developmental needs and rights because we can only see the street persona. Girls and women in the sex-trade industry are routinely victimized, which intensifies their trauma and isolation and keeps them trapped. Any minor under the age of eighteen who is involved in a commercial sex act is a victim of human trafficking.

Trafficking doesn't require movement. No borders have to be crossed. Underage youth involved in the sex trade should be considered victims, but more often than not, they're treated as criminals. The dual status of victim and offender implies agency and choice, which continues to make the responses of social services and law enforcement punitive and anemic.

The more I learned about the sex trade, the more I questioned the notion of "choice," especially when it came to adolescents or children. But even if young women did choose to prostitute themselves, did I have any less responsibility to try and help them?

As I read about the complexities of the sex trade, I felt overwhelmed. Many times I had to shut down my computer and just breathe. I felt increasingly burdened and passionate about the issue and sensed God calling me to respond in some way, to stand in the gap for those who were caught in the trap of sexual exploitation and abuse. But I wasn't sure what to do.

A few years later, I met a woman at a conference who was in charge of Late Night Outreach, part of the ministry of New Horizons, an organization founded in 1978 to reach street kids in Seattle. Its mission is to forge relationships with at-risk kids, serving and loving as Jesus did to help liberate them from life on the streets. Late Night Outreach works specifically with young women caught in prostitution, offering them emotional support, counseling, case management, school scholarships, mentoring, court advocacy, job and housing referrals, and the simple but priceless gifts of prayer and presence.

When I learned about New Horizons and Late Night Outreach, I knew that getting involved was to be my Warrior's Pose in the face of all the heartache I had been reading about. I was in. I completed the training and made a commitment to one year of outreach on Friday nights on our city streets. Every Friday I would leave our home at 7:30 in the evening to make the 8:10 ferry so I could be at a corner buzzing with prostitutes, pimps, and johns by 9:30. My companions in the ministry and I stayed outside until 3:30 on Saturday mornings—rain, shine, or bitter cold. The harm I saw on the streets soon made me fierce, like my daughter. I found myself being a warrior as I interacted with exploited women and fought for their liberation.

The most important thing I learned through this outreach is that we are all the same. The outreach is to youth up to age twenty-five, and many of the girls and women are moms. They have the same hopes and dreams for their kids that I do. They have the same desires for themselves that I do too. Many came out of the foster-care system, where abuse is rampant. Some are working for college tuition. One mom frequented the corner because her husband sent her out to earn tuition money for private education for their two daughters!

One thing is universal: All of the women and girls we encountered in the outreach had been raped as street workers. All of them. All had been scarred by violence and degradation. Sometimes I would get a glimpse of their tender side. Even though their speech could be rough and their demeanor outrageous, we met in solidarity as women. My stance became stronger even as my heart became more broken.

On the second Friday night I was to be on our corner, our team spent an hour getting baked good, snacks, coffee, tea, and hot chocolate ready. We loaded up mittens, boxes of condoms, saniwipes, and a heater so the girls could get warm. We prayed for at least half an hour before driving to our spot. Throughout the night we kept notes of how many girls we talked with and approximately how old they were, as well as how the pimps and johns were treating them. These were the things we had to offer. Often they felt so insignificant, but evil delights when we fail to hope. One of my supervisors, Sheila, herself formerly "in the trade," says that we might never know what our presence means to a young woman. We hope that somehow in the larger picture of a woman's life, it will make a difference.

Halfway through my watch that Friday night, a young, beautiful Hispanic girl charged toward our corner. "Help!" she screamed as she ran to us. "I'm going to die! Hide me!"

Even though I was new at this, I felt compelled to protect her. I had no idea whether I was shielding her from bullets, an angry pimp, or an enraged john. I just spontaneously stepped in front of her, held out my arms, and stood strong, my heart pounding. I thought that this would be an odd way to end my life, providing shelter to this girl I had never seen before.

My team leader sized up the gravity of the situation and took the young woman to our van to call one of her friends for help. Soon a car came screeching to a stop, and the girl ran and got in. I was shaken but indomitable. We had four more hours to go before returning to our computers to record our contacts. Two Fridays down, forty-six more to go!

It was an amazing privilege to do what I got to do and to begin getting to know the warrior within me. Would I continue standing strong and saying *no* to the harm that was being done? Would I accept that my tears were holy and my anger a deep shudder of rage against evil?

I had been told that volunteers in our ministry stay an average of two years. As the weeks went by, I wondered at times if I could keep doing it. It involved more than spending Friday nights on the streets. The hope, the heartache, the dreaming on behalf of these girls could be so hard to bear. It was equally hard to deal with the feelings of anger at life, laws, men, injustice, and brokenness. But as much as I wanted to quit standing on the streets and return to teaching Sunday school and volunteering with the Boys and Girls Clubs, I knew that, for that season, at least, I couldn't quit. It was too late for me to ignore the call to fight for these women. I had to help, if only in a small way. I had to do more than strike a pose. I had to reach deeper than I ever had before and ask God to strengthen my heart and steady my hands for battle.

Since ferries didn't run between 2:30 and 4:30 a.m. on Saturdays, I stayed over with my daughter Annie and her husband at their condo in downtown Seattle after volunteering. I took the elevator to the tenth floor and quietly walked into their lovely home, which had floor-to-ceiling windows facing the iconic Seattle Space Needle. The contrast between my daughter's life and the lives of those prostituted teens in our lovely city could not have been greater. In bed with very cold feet and very troubled thoughts, I pondered my heightened awareness of the haves and the have-nots.

Many of the girls I encountered on the streets were the same age and just as beautiful as my daughters, two lovely young ladies not yet thirty years old at the time, who had realized so many of their dreams. Both of them were mothers. Annie had grown her Five Element acupuncture practice, and Amanda had earned her doctorate in nursing practice. The difference between them and the women I met was that the dreams of those being sexually exploited hadn't been fulfilled. I felt that I had a responsibility to offer help and kindness and not ever judge them because of the lives they were living. Jesus has no restrictions on loving, so I followed His lead.

E lisabeth Elliot once said, "It is God to whom and with whom we travel, and while He is the end of our journey, He is also at every stopping place." A busy corner on Friday nights was my stopping place during that season of my life, and claiming the streets for His glory was what God was calling me to do.

QUESTIONS TO PONDER

Listen for echoes of your story in this essay and write about it in your journal. Then ponder the following questions and record your thoughts.

1. What kind of injustice causes your blood to boil and tears to well up in your eyes?
2. Are you reluctant to see yourself as a powerful and gifted warrior? Explain.
3. When has God cornered you, calling you to enter the fray and do something you never would have chosen to do on your own?

A Mother Like God

There are literally thousands of people around the world who have heard Jesus's plea to "feed My children." Our friend Lauran Bethell is one of them.

Ten years ago, Dan and I visited the New Life Center in Chiang Mai, Thailand, where Lauran had previously served as director. The center provides care for young, homeless girls who were trafficked into the sex-trade industry as early as age five. At the time of our visit, sixty rescued girls between the ages of nine and sixteen lived in the small complex of a few old houses, where they were provided with safe lodging, food, education, and counseling until they reached adulthood and had a viable trade to provide for themselves and their families.

Each of these girls' stories was unique. A number of parents sold their daughters to traffickers so the rest of the family could survive. Other parents were tricked into thinking their daughters were going to boarding school. Some parents even thought their children would be domestic help when in fact they were abducted and forced into the horrors of prostitution. One thing was common to all of these girls: They had suffered harm beyond comprehension and were growing up without the safe, loving arms of their mothers and fathers.

Providing care for the girls were Thai and Cambodian women who lived and worked at the facility, many of whom were trafficked girls themselves. Fe and her sister came to the New Life Center eighteen years ago and were among the first rescued girls the center embraced. Now they were glorious mothers to the other girls.

As Fe and her sister walked Dan and me through the center, I felt as though I was on holy ground. On the walls of one of the sewing rooms were pictures the girls had drawn. We asked Fe the meaning of the words by the drawings, and it broke my heart to hear her read some of the captions.

"A child has a right to live at home."
"A child has a right to go to school."
"A child has a right not to be abused."

Yes, that's how it should be, and how it was for my daughters. Why is it that my girls had the home, school, and safety those girls wrote about having a right to experience? It was neither comprehensible nor fair that these precious girls didn't have mothers delighting in them throughout their young lives.

After we toured the facility, we were shown to an area outside where we would eat lunch with the girls and the house mothers. While we waited for the food to be served, I had the joy of engaging with eight-year-old Asha, a girl with gorgeous eyes; dark, sleek hair; and huge dimples when she smiled. She won my heart within minutes. We began laughing and chasing each other around the yard. She ran to a large tree with orange flowers and, with bare feet, climbed swiftly and expertly to a very high branch and grabbed a brown pod of some sort as she smiled down on me mischievously. Then she shimmied down as quickly as she had climbed up, and I marveled at her skill and balance and joy.

We laughed and chased each other a bit longer until it was time to wash our hands in tin basins by the water pump. Then Dan and I sat down at the table with fifteen little girls and three house mothers. After we prayed and the dishes of food had been passed around, Asha handed Dan a small piece of fruit from the pod she had brought down from the tree.

One of the house mothers asked, "Do you like spicy food?" Dan said yes and took a small taste, then handed it to me to taste. He acted as if it was fine and didn't react in any way to shield me from the shock that was awaiting me. I took a bite and almost went crazy with how hot it was. The laughter around the table was boisterous with delight. Asha was laughing the loudest. Everyone had fun watching my antics of clamoring for water to take away the burning sensation. I don't think I have ever been in more pain eating something so spicy!

When it was time for Dan and me to leave, we took photos, and Asha ran to stand next to me. She was so like my own daughters, who would often seek to win the affection of a new houseguest. To this day I consider Asha's behavior toward me an honor. I think about her often and wonder how she is doing and what she is doing. I'm grateful that she received love and care at the New Life Center, which has been helping children in need for thirty years now. I'm also grateful for our friend Lauran. But until I met Asha, I didn't realize that my face, hands, and presence could offer other children besides my own a chance to experience being mothered. I'll always be grateful to her for that.

The prophet Isaiah said, "For a long time I have kept silent, I have been quiet and held myself back. But now, like a woman in childbirth, I cry out, I gasp and pant" (Isaiah 42:14). The language is similar to Paul's words in Romans 8, where he described the birth pangs of hope. All of creation is in childbirth, he wrote. All of us, male and female.

> We know that the whole creation has been groaning as in the pains of childbirth right up to the present time. Not only so, but we ourselves, who have the first fruits of the Spirit, groan inwardly as we wait eagerly for our adoption to sonship, the redemption of our bodies. For in this hope we were saved. But hope that is seen is no hope at all. Who hopes for what they already have? But if we hope for what we do not yet have, we wait for it patiently. In the same way, the Spirit helps us in our weakness. We do not know what we ought to pray for, but the Spirit himself intercedes for us through wordless groans. (verses 22–26)

Like a woman about to give birth, my God groans with deep heartache for the motherless girls I met in Chiang Mai. God also sings over them with a lullaby and gently rocks them to sleep (Zephaniah 3:17). God wails and delights over them. I am called to do the same.

It took me far too many years to realize that God is revealed in Scripture not only as a father but also as a mother. And it took even longer to understand what that means for my way of being on this earth. Because of Asha, I have new eyes to see that I am called to be a mother like God, to prize groaning and singing in every situation and with every one of God's children I meet.

Questions to Ponder

Listen for echoes of your story in this essay and write about it in your journal. Then ponder the following questions and record your thoughts.

1. Describe a time when your mothering brought you unexpected goodness.
2. In what way does God's self-portrayal as a mother change your understanding of God?
3. Has playfulness ever landed you in hot water? How so?

Burnout

The afternoon turned black at 4:35 p.m. It was dark as night as the winter rain pounded on our roof with a vengeance for hours before I left for the ferry. Rain gear over layers of warm clothing and a winter coat, boots, and an umbrella were my armor as I trudged from relative protection from the elements to meet our Late Night Outreach team for another night on the streets of Seattle.

It was a slow night. Only seventeen women came to get hot drinks and talk. The johns were few, and hardly any pimps were out. Who would want to be hanging out in this cold, monsoon-like rain if they didn't have to? One of our favorite girls came by and talked about her desire to leave the track. Janell was twenty-one years old and had been involved in prostitution for more than six years. And she was one of the "older" women! We prayed with her, asking that she would have the strength to leave her current profession and make a new start. She wanted to go to community college, so we mentioned the scholarship money available to her.

I hoped with a hope that ached that she really would leave the track. She wanted to the previous year and sounded determined to make it happen. We didn't see her often after that, but once was too much if she intended to leave the game. It felt strange to welcome all the girls while really wishing that we wouldn't see them again.

The few women I have personally known who have left the track required a churchload of people and a boatload of professionals to help them change their lifestyles. It is for this reason that burnout is so great among those who work to liberate them. The successes are few and slow.

Cory was only one of the younger women on our team who was taking up the gauntlet and fighting for social awareness, justice, and redemption. She was twenty-one years old and a senior in college, and that night with us on the street was her first. She had wanted to join our team since she was fifteen! How amazing is that?

I knew almost nothing about prostitution when I was her age and probably thought it didn't exist in our city. It was the very last thing on my mind. Instead, I was thinking about hiking the Grand Canyon or backpacking in Europe when I was twenty-one. If there were groups helping prostituted children, women, and men get off the streets at the time, I didn't know about them.

It encourages me to see the passion of the twenty-something generation to stand for justice. Women like Cory, Jennifer, and Kelly go on mission trips around the world, volunteering with street ministries that exist to help disadvantaged people have better lives and opportunities. I love these young women's zeal to serve and help. I am energized and hopeful because of their love. Sometimes, however, their passion takes a toll, as it did in Kelly's life.

Kelly was a senior in college and served on various committees that dealt with social-justice issues. Committed to reaching out to girls on the street for some time, she freely gave her cell-phone number to our girls and took their numbers as well. In the course of befriending two of our girls, she became overwhelmed with the injustices that had befallen them and began a downward spiral. Incompletes in her college courses became more the norm than the exception. She eventually became ill and was unable to remain on our team. It was heartbreaking to see how ill-equipped a privileged white girl was to confront the violence in the lives of those two street girls.

During those years volunteering with Late Night Outreach, I was often asked, "How do you keep from taking this home with you? Don't you worry about how all this suffering will affect you?" I have known many people who try to compartmentalize their lives, but it never worked for me. As a privileged white woman, I sleep in a world that is as far from the track as the earth is from the sun. It was easy to feel like a fake out there—a newbie who sincerely wanted to help but knew I couldn't hold back the tide of human suffering and sin. And then when I returned to my suburban world, it felt thin and indulgent at times as I visited cool coffee shops, quaint eateries, and niche boutiques. I ached in one world; I struggled in the other. Truthfully, I have never felt fully at home in either world. In fact, the track, as raw, dark, and heartbreaking as it is, often felt closer to the truth than my so-called happier world.

The apostle James said, "Grieve, mourn and wail. Change your laughter to mourning and your joy to gloom. Humble yourselves before the Lord, and he will lift you up" (James 4:9–10). His words are strange and counterintuitive. We all want to turn our tears into laughter and gloom into joy. Yet James invites us to embrace sorrow and let Jesus raise us from the ashes of our grief.

That night in Seattle, I felt burned out. It wasn't merely the gloom of the Northwest winter that had me down, even though I knew it wasn't helping. It was more my awareness of how unfair it was that I am rich and my new friends were not only poor but were also violated and used. Sometimes it was more than I could bear. I grieved, mourned, and wailed inside every time I stood on that dark street corner handing out condoms and hot chocolate. I couldn't rid the world of the injustice. I could do little to help other than share in the suffering and brokenness of these young women and trust that redemption lay ahead.

The long haul in this kind of ministry is nothing to balk at. This is grueling and draining work if not cloaked in prayer and approached with realistic goals. I was constantly aware that burnout was just around the corner for me if I forgot that this was God's fight. I was only required to show up bearing kindness.

QUESTIONS TO PONDER

Listen for echoes of your story in this essay and write about it in your journal. Then ponder the following questions and record your thoughts.

1. Describe a moment or season when you felt you simply couldn't keep going.
2. How did your exhaustion or discouragement in one area bleed into other parts of your life?
3. Entering your grief is required to disrupt burnout. What keeps you from tending to your sorrow?

Risking Wildly

My husband is a lover of fly-fishing. Years ago my Colorado friend Lauren called me and said, "Let's give our husbands an Orvis fly-fishing weekend and get lessons with them."

It was a wild and wonderful time with personal guides in the deep canyons of Colorado—the guides who knew where the fish were. Brilliant! I recall the sunlight and fresh air and the thrill of the catch as if it were yesterday.

The best part of the weekend was watching my husband come alive and be a different man when he donned his fishing apparel and dove into the adventure with crazy delight. Never in his life had he loved a sport more. As for me, I felt like a child when I walked through the water with my waders on. Better said, I felt like a boy-child who got to play in puddles and streams. I was as captivated as Dan was!

Some years up the road, Dan planned for us to spend part of his sabbatical in New Zealand, a mecca for fly-fishermen. It turned out to be the scariest adventure of my life! We arrived with two suitcases and two huge duffel bags filled with enough gear to get us through the next three months. Dan had arranged for a rental car, but it didn't work out once we got there. With much trepidation, I put my faith in my husband's ability to drive a bright-red BMW motorcycle on the left-hand side of the road!

If you look at an atlas, you'll see how many mountains there are in New Zealand. Roads over mountains mean many switchbacks. The speed limits for the turns range from eighty-five kilometers per hour (Kiwis love to drive fast!) to fifteen kilometers. Maneuvering is tricky when you're lugging three fishing rods, two sets of waders, boots, two laptop computers, cameras, clothes, rain gear, and, yes, books. And did I say that I usually had on five to six layers of clothing? The wind never stopped blowing, often gusting at speeds up to fifty miles per hour. Every peak we climbed traumatized me.

When we made it to the top of one mountain, I literally crawled on all fours to a large rock and wrapped my arms around it as if clinging to it for dear life. Dan had to coax me to let go when it was time to make our way downhill. I was terrified that the wind would blow us off the highway. Once as we were coming around a switchback turn, our motorcycle literally stopped because of the force of the wind!

New Zealanders are wild risk takers. They go whitewater rafting without rafts! I am not kidding. They put on a helmet and float down the roaring waters feet first. When one boat rams into another boat during a sailing regatta, they just stuff something in the hole and keep sailing until the race is over. Americans backpack for a few months; the Kiwis take off backpacking for a year or two! They're the most friendly, fun-loving people to travel with and are always ready to down a drink with you.

This beautiful country is unlike any place I have ever been. It has four million people and forty million sheep. You never know when a thousand sheep might be crossing the road. As a sea of white passes in front of you, you had better be patient and enjoy the scenery!

Everything the Kiwis do is over the top. So you can imagine my surprise when a 250-pound Maori woman who was coloring my roots said she would not let me leave the salon if I went along with my husband's plan to motorcycle over the "southern Alps" on the way to Aoraki Mount Cook National Park.

"The island will not be kind to you," she told me. "No one goes during the snowy season on a motorbike. You will never make it out alive! I will talk to your husband about his faulty and fool-hardy thinking."

Of course, when she talked with Dan, he agreed with her that it was dangerous, but he just crossed his fingers behind his back, letting this strong woman think she had won the argument. All too soon we were traveling through wind, rain, snow, and sleet. Only once did Dan get confused about which side of the rode to drive on. It was on a roundabout when we came face-to-face with a tour bus. Thankfully both vehicles had good brakes!

Dan and I traveled for more than three months on the North and South Islands of this wild and beautiful country. That may not sound so strange until I tell you that we had never been together that many days in a row. The entire time, I counted fewer than thirty motor-bikes on the road!

If you've ever seen photographs of the South Island, you like-ly noticed beautiful sheep paddocks with hedges for boundaries. Those hedges are actually trees that are carved by huge machinery twice a year and sometimes stand thirty feet tall and ten feet deep. (Hint: This is more about keeping the wind out than keeping the livestock in!)

While on the South Island, we fished in countless beautiful streams and rivers. I understood the local fly-fishing pamphlets better once I had to fish in the wind. On the pamphlet were pho-tographs of fishermen ducking behind hedges to cast a line. It was on one of those cold, windy days that we found ourselves wondering whether we should call it quits for the day. Dan had

had a couple of strikes, but I'd had nothing and was getting discouraged. He decided to put a different fly on my rod and then pointed me upstream.

After casting only a few times, I was surprised when something hit my fly. It was so strong that I hollered to Dan that it was most likely a log that wasn't budging. I kept trying to reel it in and was shocked that it started moving. Dan whooped and hollered with glee as he watched me fight and work the line back and forth and out and in. Whatever was on my hook was a monster!

Becky fishing wildly in New Zealand

Fifteen minutes later, Dan was next to me with his net and scooped a thirty-one-inch, beautiful spotted-brown trout out of the river. I had just caught Dan's dream fish!

My husband has fished a thousand times more often than I have, and he has never caught a trout as large as mine. I love fly-fishing, but I'd rather curl up with a good book. He loves fly-fishing just slightly less than he loves me and his children and grandchildren. He has already stipulated that his remains be released in his favorite Montana river. The look of pride on his face when he netted my monster trout was equal only to the look of dejection that he hadn't caught the fish himself.

Becky Fly Fishing

How many looks will be remembered over a lifetime? I have no idea. I do know that for all the turns, twists, rises, and falls of our life story together, no moment will feel like a more playful gift than when God let me pose for a picture with my prize-winning brown trout. The catch was almost worth the risk of the insane journey it took to get there. I can't help but think of how true that often is on our wild, windy ride toward eternity.

QUESTIONS TO PONDER

Listen for echoes of your story in this essay and write about it in your journal. Then ponder the following questions and record your thoughts.

1. Write about a moment of risk that opened the door to God's delight. Describe it in detail.
2. Most of life is lived reasonably. In what areas of your life do you yearn to take an unchartered path? Whose voice warns you against taking wild risks?
3. How might you incorporate more risks in your life?

Take Off Your Shoes

It was an amazing invitation, and I almost said no. Our third child was in first grade, and I was invited to go fly-fishing with my husband and his friends in Cheesman Canyon, one of the most beautiful canyons in Colorado. Was it really okay to sneak away on a Tuesday in September? It seemed an extravagant way to spend a school day, but I said yes.

I crammed my gear in the back of the SUV and squeezed next to my husband in the backseat, the lone woman with four men. We drove on winding mountain roads and found a skimpy place to park on a slanted opening on a red dirt road in the middle of nowhere. The river was a steep fifty-minute hike away with all of our gear. Why had I thought this would be fun?

Once we got near the river, I took off my hiking boots and began the process of putting on my felted boots over neoprene waders and my fly-fishing vest on top of five other layers. The air was crisp; the river was fast. The men took off to fish in various spots along the river, and I knew that for safety reasons, I would stay close to my husband. I put on my Polaroid sunglasses and felt like an imposter.

As Dan and I began to make our way into the current, I was impressed that I didn't slip on the mossy rocks while trying to keep up with him. I can't recall if I even got to cast. What I do recall is that the river was deep and swift, and water that Dan could wade in with his 220-pound frame was disastrous for me with 100 fewer pounds. Before I knew it, my chest was propelled beyond my feet, and there I went, rushing forward down the freezing-cold current with water filling my waders and a siren going off in my brain. I tried to stay calm as I looked ahead and assessed the danger. I was mercifully near a bend in the river, and branches became my only hope of saving myself. The rocks I crashed into were my friends. I grabbed them and held on silently, too afraid to scream.

Eventually I clawed my way to the bank as my frantic husband caught up with me. He sat with me until I told him he needed to go back to the river and fish. We both knew the other men were by that point far away in different directions, and it would be at least five hours before we would all trek back up the canyon to our SUV. I knew I had to get my wet clothes off and try to get warm with what little sunlight was reaching the canyon floor. I could endure lots, but hypothermia is a stealthy enemy.

I found a skimpy bush and framed some of my wet clothes around me for insulation. Sitting there shivering in my underpants, I tried desperately not to cry as the bone-numbing cold gnawed at my body. The pain was debilitating!

I remembered feeling that way after our third child was born by C-section. I had an inguinal hernia that made me feel as if the surgeon had left a couple pairs of scissors in my abdomen. I stayed in the hospital for nine days because I also developed a stabbing cough.

My mother came to help for a week when I returned home, but she busied herself with house projects, such as washing all the curtains and organizing all the closets. She would forget to bring me water or meals as I lay in bed, incapacitated with pain. Nursing Andrew and combing our seven-year-old's long hair before the school bus came took all the energy I had. Dan was away at a seminar, and three-year-old Amanda had an ear infection. It was too painful to ask my mother to tend to me.

Sometimes evil still tries to make me feel unworthy and invisible, but I'm transitioning into a new phase of life. I just returned from the biannual gathering of the International Christian Alliance on Prostitution (ICAP) in Wisconsin. In the past I went as a caregiver to the exploited and as an intercessor in prayer, but this time I went as a trained coleader of a "story group." I joined four other facilitators and asked the same questions the Lord asked Hagar in Genesis 16:8: "Where have you come from, and where are you going?" Research shows that when victims are able to share their stories of trauma with a caring person or group, healing can follow in life-transforming ways.

I cofacilitated a group with Abby, a graduate from the Seattle School who is on the Allender Center teaching staff. In our group were four women from three different countries. Two of them were American missionaries helping girls who were prostituted in brothels or on the streets. The other two women had previously been involved in prostitution and were now helping others get off the streets. It takes great courage for the participants in our story groups to share painful stories with strangers and explore how shame and trauma have marked their style of relating and choice of relationships and careers. The group members stand on the front lines of battle as we fight a war against evil with each person.

Our contact person in Ethiopia, who started a ministry to prostituted women in Addis Ababa, once told us that Africans don't like to tell sad stories. Leaders, especially, don't tell their sad stories because it lowers their status in the group. Even with this information, we still wanted to offer a safe group setting for helpers and victims alike to share their trauma and heartache. People in the helping professions hear many painful stories, and because of this, they suffer what is called *vicarious trauma*. They, too, need to talk, and they, too, carry their own stories of trauma. Often, the stories the Allender Center team focuses on are those within the participants' families of origin.

In our groups, the leaders read their stories first, and the rest of the group listens and then interacts according to preset guidelines. To be able to speak without anyone interrupting and with only kind eyes and engaged people listening is an experience of extravagant care. It's as if everyone takes off their shoes before entering this safe, caring time with safe, skilled guides.

The week was filled with heartbreaking stories. The participants came to their group with a written story of about one thousand words. Everyone had the opportunity to read their stories without interruption. While someone is reading, there is no advice giving or confrontation. We watch the reader's face and afterward ask about what she was feeling as she read certain parts. We might notice her word choice or where she felt absent or present while reading. We focus on each person for about twenty minutes, and the results are remarkable to behold.

The privilege of telling my own story in such a safe group has healed me in ways I never could have imagined. I had no idea how good it would feel to have others care for me so skillfully and tenderly. I began with some skepticism but ended up hooked. After being trained as a facilitator, I now feel qualified to enter this arena of trauma work with others. It has been the most unexpected journey of my life. I have seen so many students at the Seattle School arrive one way and leave completely different. I was envious of their freedom and didn't know how to get in line to experience it myself. It was always bittersweet when I traveled with my husband to hear him teach and watch people begin to heal before my eyes. Frankly, "What about me?" was the cry of my heart; I was furious that I was left out of the circle and didn't know how to get in. All of that envy is gone now. I have received so much care from really good and wise facilitators, and it has changed my life.

Sometimes what I'm called to do is as scary as being taken down a strong current in a freezing river. But to step on the neck of evil on behalf of others is wildly holy and crazy fun as I see the weight of burdens people have carried for years slip to the ground. Jesus has asked me to take off my shoes as I enter the holiness of others' stories of tragedy, as well as my own, and honor them. I hope I will always be willing to step into the water and see where it takes me next. Wherever the Spirit of God throws me, I may land shivering on shore and want to hide, but with what I know now, I will wade back into the river.

QUESTIONS TO PONDER

Listen for echoes of your story in this essay and write about it in your journal. Then ponder the following questions and record your thoughts.

1. Not all risks turn out well. Which risks have you regretted taking? How did these regrets mark your future?
2. When has fear prevented you from truly hearing the pain of another person's story?
3. When you think of stepping on the neck of evil, how does that make your body feel?

Waiting for Donna

It was a proverbial dark and stormy night when our Late Night Outreach team arrived in downtown Seattle to meet our girls in the pouring rain. We had baked Thanksgiving treats and individually wrapped each one, but it was raining too hard to pass them out unless our girls were in their own cars or leaving the track for the night.

Our parkas began soaking through early in the evening, and our two umbrellas weren't enough to cover our team of six. We fantasized about how we would rig an awning over our little corner.

Half of the women we encountered carried their own umbrellas, and when they didn't have one, we held ours over their heads. One woman came with a tattered umbrella that looked as if a truck had run over it. She looked darling but funny, and we all laughed at what remained of her sole defense against the weather. She said her boots were completely soaked, and her toes were squishing inside.

The highlight of my evening was seeing Donna again. The week before, she had graced us with a bit of her story. It was so sad that I knew it would haunt me for a very long time.

Donna was a petite African American woman with a mature beauty beyond her eighteen years. Social services took her away from home at the age of three after her stepsister, who was thirteen years older, reported to her school teacher that her father was raping her little sister. Donna had no memory of any sexual abuse. She was in the foster-care system for a year and then went to live with grandparents, who wanted a life of travel and leisure and paid the neighbors $800 a month to let Donna live with them. Since her ethnicity was different from those in her school and neighborhood, she grew up tough. At twelve she began turning tricks and dropped out of school at the age of fourteen because she was bored. Even alternative schools didn't challenge her.

Years later, as a young adult, Donna hoped to reconnect with her family, whom she hadn't seen since she was five years old. So far her relatives had refused to see her. I couldn't imagine what it would be like to have a family who didn't want to see me again, or forgot that I even existed. I wondered what it was like for her to be alone on the streets.

The web of abuse, control, and "love" young women like Donna experience is unimaginable to me. Even though their pimps beat and rape them, our girls still say they love them and would never trust the courts or someone in social services over their pimps. The idea of leaving the life they know is scarier than longing for a life they want. All these young women have dreams. When we ask them what they hope to be doing in five or ten years, they never talk about what they're doing now. Never.

It's easy for those of us with families, friends, homes, and careers to judge their lifestyles. But who are we to judge a beautiful woman who lost her family as a toddler? What does normalcy mean when you're alone, black, and have to be tough as nails to survive first grade? I cannot imagine the hardening of heart that was required of Donna to survive that kind of abandonment. How did she treat me with respect and kindness? I think if I had been on the track, I would have hated me.

That cold night Donna had wrapped a wool scarf around her head in a fashion that was really cute. I told her I'd never seen anyone wear a scarf like that and wondered why we all didn't do it! It was a fun, sweet moment of connection that led to a brief discussion about her dinner the night before. She told me she'd spent twenty-two dollars on a meal while out with a potential john. The potato salad had been good, but the chicken had been tough. She said that it had been a waste of an evening, and she hadn't made any money. She brought up the amount she had spent on her dinner two more times, and I found myself saying, "I'm sorry about your evening. I hope that tomorrow night will be better for you. But let me say, you are so worth twenty-two dollars. You are so, so worth that, and I only wish your chicken had been more tasty."

A group of us started asking one another when our birthdays were, and Donna said that hers was coming up in a few weeks. I calmly (with my heart beating fast) asked if I could have her phone number and suggested we meet for a meal to celebrate her twenty-first birthday. To my delight she said yes, so now I had her number! I hoped that we would meet and begin to hear more of each other's stories. For me, it would be a new way of stepping out in faith and trusting God for His grace and love.

As excited as I was at first to have Donna's number, I didn't call her all week long. I was too afraid. My coworkers were elated when they got a phone number, and they called without hesitation. I, on the other hand, kept busy and chose not to take the risk. So much hope and fear were wrapped up in my budding relationship with Donna. I think it was the same for her.

The following week I was thrilled when she came by again. She said that Thursday nights were the best time to go to dinner, but she wouldn't make eye contact with me. I was disappointed when she abruptly ended our conversation. Before our team packed up to leave for the night, I approached her and gave her a good-bye hug. "I'm still looking forward to your birthday dinner," I said, and this time she looked at me, if ever so briefly.

Over the following few weeks, more than twenty-five calls went into arranging this celebratory outing. As the day approached, Donna asked me to call her on the morning of our dinner in case she forgot about our date. Unfortunately I awakened her when I called. She asked me to call again so she wouldn't forget, and I promised I would. An hour before I left for the ferry, I called and got a phone recording that said, "I dropped my phone in the water. If you don't hear back from me, that's why."

Obviously, her phone was just fine, given her voice-mail message. Was this a way of telling me, "Get lost"? Did I really want to get on the ferry on a night other than my "obligatory" Friday and walk fifteen blocks in the rain to our meeting place? Did I really want to spend hours away from what I could be doing given the now-uncertain prospect of our dining together? Why had I wrapped up gifts and written powerfully affirming sentences on the most beautiful card I had waited two years to use? Should I just forget about trying to connect with her? *No*, I thought. *I choose to be at peace even if Donna doesn't show. I choose to remain faithful and hopeful.*

Parking spaces downtown were nearly nonexistent, but I finally found one and ran blocks to the ferry. Dripping with sweat, I called Donna again once I found a seat. No answer. I walked the fifteen blocks to our designated meeting place, sat down, and called again. This time I left her a message saying that I was fine if she didn't come, and I hoped she was with someone who loved her. I wanted her to know that I would look forward to another time when I could take her out for dinner. Then it occurred to me that Jesus never says to us,

"Why didn't you show up? I was waiting for you!" Why would I be mad at being inconvenienced if Donna was a no-show? While waiting for Donna, I finally grasped what it means to give love freely. It's really pretty simple. We're called to love, not judge. The Bible says that Jesus came to love and save the world, not to condemn it (John 3:17). How wonderful.

We didn't need to judge our girls or tell them what to do. If a young woman wanted our help to finish her GED or get counseling on how to care for her baby, then we could offer it. Meanwhile, our role was to love unconditionally, the way Jesus loved us, too. It is by love that God draws His children. It is by love that we know we are His beloved and are perfect in His sight. It was freeing to interact with the girls on the track as an ambassadors of love rather than judgment. I didn't have to be the change or the hope. The Holy Spirit was the one who would work in their lives as I listened to His leading. How glorious to be His hands and feet!

Sitting in the restaurant waiting for Donna, I felt overwhelmed with God's kindness in countless ways I will never see and, even if I do, never comprehend. Rather than going straight home, I went to the art museum and bought an annual membership with a guest pass. There was a children's room at the museum with the biggest wooden puzzle you could imagine. The lobby was beautiful, with windows and lovely seating. The restaurant was grand, and the gift shop was amazing. And the art was, well, exquisite beyond belief. I yearned for Donna to be my guest there. I got carried away thinking about meeting her there throughout the year. I could see the seasons change in my mind as I envisioned us talking and just hanging out together.

I admit that it aches to dream for girls like Donna, to wait expectantly for what God can do in their lives. One of the hardest things about being involved in this ministry was hoping for and wanting so much for these women. It was costly in ways I hadn't calculated before I began. The longing for connection and redemption could be excruciating at times, as so few of our deepest desires came to fruition.

But at what price do we relinquish our dreams, even if their chances of coming true are slim? I choose to keep hoping, to keep loving. Jesus says that we find Him by losing our lives for others. It's true.

As I gave my time and my heart to the girls on the street, I received far more from them in return. I think I learned more about love from entering their world than in any other place I've ever been. For me, there was no other choice but to continue dreaming and hoping and praying.

QUESTIONS TO PONDER

Listen for echoes of your story in this essay and write about it in your journal. Then ponder the following questions and record your thoughts.

1. Have you ever been friends with a person who was extremely different from you? Write about the experience.
2. Have you ever gone out of your way to show someone you cared? If so, did you regret the time it took out of your schedule, or did you end up receiving more than you gave?
3. What is your deepest reluctance to surrender to love?

The Bosom of Jesus

It was almost April, and one news station reported that our city had had a mere forty hours of sunlight since October. It had been the darkest five months of my life. Record-breaking rainfall had been our plight that year. Even the interior of my car seemed soggy. However, when I opened my eyes that morning, there was hope of a sunny day. By the time Dan joined me downstairs, the house was filled with sunshine. We soaked in the rays like turtles on a mossy rock.

We usually took a local hike, but that day Dan had a different plan. We drove to Fort Ward to walk along the shoreline. Joy was in the air! It was evident, as people were out in droves drinking in the sun. Dan and I walked hand in hand like lovers and even greeted strangers. It was a glorious time.

When we returned home, the phone rang. I listened to Dan answer it and knew immediately that it was Sondra, Dan's childhood neighbor who had power of attorney for his mother's health care. Jo had been failing over the past seven years, and that afternoon Sondra told Dan that she had taken a turn for the worse. The day changed in an instant. I sighed and in my mind could hear my father say, "There is never a good time for death."

When Dan's father died in 1991, Dan said that he had joined a club no one really wants to be in.

"What club are you talking about?" I asked.

"The dead parents club," he answered.

Unless you're a member, it's a club you cannot understand. Since losing my own parents, I know the heartache is real. I miss them more now than when they were alive, and I long to see them again in heaven.

Dan and I arrived in Columbus, Ohio, at four thirty the next afternoon, and when we walked into the memory-care facility where Jo had been living for the past two weeks, everyone seemed to know who we were. A nurse came to us and said that she hadn't thought Jo would make it through the night. "She's been waiting for you."

The nurse opened the door and introduced us to Veronica, a sitter from Ghana. Immediately I knew that she was a believer. Dan and I went to Jo's bedside, her emaciated body looking like a small child's frame under a white quilt. She seemed at peace, and when Dan touched her head and greeted her, her breathing changed. I stroked her hair and told her I loved her and how beautiful she was even now. Once again, she wasn't able to do anything but breathe a bit differently, but we knew that she heard us.

Our children called to say their last good-byes to their grandmother, and the holiness of the words they spoke also caused Jo's breathing to change. Her spirit told our spirits that she had comprehended their farewells. Wayne, her partner, was in a wheelchair next to her bedside, his eyes vacant. We loved on him, knowing his loss was much greater than ours. We spent the next three hours together in a place where the veil was torn aside more than it normally is.

After hearing about the condition of Dan's mother, the president of the Seattle School had e-mailed Dan, "Let your heart find all the peace that you can." The dean of students had also e-mailed. "Make sure you ask for forgiveness," he advised, "and make sure you grant your mother forgiveness for what she needs forgiveness for." With those mens' orders, Dan was valiant and prepared.

I left the room with Wayne and Veronica so that Dan could be alone with his mom. When we returned, I could tell that all that needed to be said had been said. Then it was my turn. I told Jo that I loved her and thanked her for being a good mother-in-law. I said other true words that rolled easily off my tongue, and I meant every one. We then joined hands with Veronica and sang and prayed over the shell of this ninety-three-year-old mother. Veronica closed our time together, and I felt as if angels had already arrived in the room. It was the right time to leave.

Dan's phone awakened us the next morning. It was Veronica calling to tell us that ten minutes earlier, at 8:47 a.m., Jo had "passed unto the blessed bosom of Jesus."

I looked at Dan, and he said, "I'm at peace. I said everything I wanted to say, and I have no regrets for not being there when she died."

I couldn't help but think that our being present would have been an intrusion. If I could choose any guide to escort me from this world to the next, I would choose Veronica to sing me into the arms of Jesus and my family. I was at peace too.

The rest of the day unfolded with heavenly provision. A morning service was arranged, and we were seated in the Buckeye Room. Dan thanked Sondra and Wayne for their care of Jo, and I thanked the administrative staff and nurses for their kind care as well. We all told a few stories about Jo that brought laughter and tears. Then Steve, the hospice chaplain, gave one of the greatest sermons on love and faith that I have ever heard. Each psalm, passage, and prayer was sustenance to my heart and a glorious testimony to Jesus's death, resurrection, and ascension. Dan had planned on speaking, but halfway through the service, he heard God say, "Just be a son and receive." He breathed into the realization that he was released from a lifetime of caring for his mother. It was a new day.

After the service, we went with Sondra to Jo's room to gather her outfit for the funeral home. We hugged Sondra and Wayne good-bye and walked out to our rental car. The sun was shining, and the outside world beckoned. With an hour to kill before meeting with bank trustees, Dan asked, "What do you want to do?" I knew in an instant exactly what we should do. When I told Dan, it rang true with him as well.

We drove to where the bakery of Dan's father used to be and on the property's sidewalk shared communion with a chocolate-chip cookie and black coffee. Both cookie and coffee were favorites of my mother-in-law. With these fitting elements, we brought closure to Jo's life and partook of the sweetness Dan's father and mother had given him. With tears of gratitude, we ate and drank and remembered an imperfect but loved woman whom we will one day get to see in all her splendor.

What is a life? What is a life well lived? What remains when we have passed into the blessed bosom of Jesus? Dan's mother gave life and at times took life from my husband. There were times I couldn't bear her. There were times her laughter brought so much joy. She was the mother of the man I love, and without her I wouldn't have known the love I do as a wife, mother, and grandmother.

As I stood outside my father-in-law's bakery contemplating Jo's life and death, I was filled with gratitude for what her life meant to me, for how I had learned to love her in spite of her faults, and for the assurance that I will one day meet her again in a realm where all conflict, disappointment, and heartache will be wiped away. When I'm gathered into the arms of Jesus one day, I imagine that my children will have similar thoughts and feelings. I hope they'll feast on the reality of what He has done for us all and be at peace with the bittersweetness of their loss. I am their mother, imperfect but loved, and I know we'll dance together one sweet day in glory.

QUESTIONS TO PONDER

Listen for echoes of your story in this essay and write about it in your journal. Then ponder the following questions and record your thoughts.

1. What do you hope people will say about you after your death?
2. Has a loved one's death inspired you to live your life more fully? In what way?
3. The day of restoration is coming when we will be with Jesus and dance together in glory. How does that realization change your heart? Your relationships? The way you treat your body?

The Final Doorway

This was it. The beginning of the end.

As the airplane circled over my hometown of Columbus, Ohio, I couldn't stop the tears from flowing. My dad had been in a depression for four months and was choosing to die. He was having trouble swallowing and had aspirated food into his lungs, which led to pneumonia and being admitted to the hospital. Doctors put in a feeding tube to try to nourish his depleted body, but it didn't help.

My sister and I knew that my mother's dementia and cruelty toward my father was a hurdle too difficult for him to jump over at this point in his life. Getting better wouldn't change his wife's demeanor. I had suggested separating them and having each parent live with a different child, but my father wasn't willing to do that, knowing it would be too hard on my mother. And now he had lost his will to live.

Could my body and heart bear what was ahead? My mantra became "God before me, God beneath me, God behind me, God above me, God beside me." The plane touched down, and I dried my tears.

I arrived at Riverside Methodist Hospital and slept in the bed next to my dad's while we waited for a hospice transfer to Kobacker House. I was amazed that the hospital staff allowed me to sleep in the room, but when they heard that his father had fallen in the night and died years before, they had compassion for my dad's fear of being alone and let me stay close to him.

We watched the news together and some nights in the wee hours, we found *Sky King* and *Shirley Temple's Storybook* reruns. Our words were few. For three days, the late-afternoon sun would shine on my bed, where I sat under the covers to stay warm in the cold room. I soaked in every ray while we waited for our food trays to come.

My brother-in-law brought my mother to visit during the day, and Trinity United Methodist Church sent a minister every day to pray with and comfort us. Longtime friends of my parents also showed up as we waited for the next step. Previously, three physicians told my father that they could fix him so he could live longer. With what little strength he had left, my father pounded his fist on the bed and said, "NO!" He knew what he wanted, and we honored that.

Finally, hospice paperwork was approved, orders were given, and the attendants came to take my dad by ambulance to his last "home." His wish to have only ice chips to eat had been granted. Little did I know that it would take nineteen days for him to die!

His hospice room became the most sacred room of my life so far. It was a sanctuary of love. I set up my CD player and played Kathy Troccoli's worship music. I had peppermint and clove essential oils to fortify myself and set my Bible and my beloved copy of *The One Year Book of Hymns* devotional next to the recliner at my father's bedside. The peace of the room and hallowedness of the hallways allowed my body and heart to rest alongside my father.

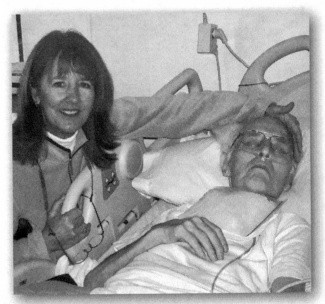

Becky and her dad in hospice

The mission in hospice was so different from the hospital. I had never witnessed such kindness before. The hospice nurses acknowledged my presence and loved on my dad in tender ways I've never seen before or since. They lovingly touched him and asked what he needed. They all called him "beautiful Paul" and spoke of his gorgeous "Paul Newman blue eyes." As I watched their care, I saw my dad become a young Paul again in his dying body, childlike as he received their tender loving care.

One day the volunteers at Kobacker House helped me bundle him up and wheel him outside in his bed so he could feel the warm sunshine on his face. It was another ending: the last time to be outside with my father.

Childhood friends, his and mine, came to sit with him. Time stood still as my father's legacy played out in Technicolor before my eyes. Even though he had been retired for fifteen years, his former brokerage-firm colleagues came and stayed for an entire day. My father could barely speak anymore, but it didn't matter, because his friends and colleagues were simply there to testify to the kindness they had received during the years they worked or played with him.

I left the hospice facility each day to walk the streets of Grandview Heights, his childhood community. I meandered down countless sidewalks around the neighborhood. I looked at every house wondering if my dad had delivered newspapers to those porches twice a day between the ages of twelve and seventeen. I wondered which neighbors wrote letters to him when he was stationed in Europe and North Africa during World War II. I thought about his childhood friend who died of gangrene after a hardball hit his leg while he was playing baseball. Where had he lived? And where was the home of the boy who lived with his grandparents because he was a seventh child, and his parents had too many others to feed in Chicago? Why had I not walked these streets and asked these questions when my dad was still able to come with me? Why had I not been more curious about his life?

I've marked in my devotional hymnal every hymn I sang to my dad during those last days. I wanted to be reminded of all the times I stood next to him in a pew singing those songs. In my mind I was hearing his strong, beautiful voice singing words of faith. I ached as I sang alone and with my sister and brother in that hospice room. In our almost-tone-deaf voices, we belted out, without shame, "Turn Your Eyes upon Jesus," "Be Thou My Vision," and "Fairest Lord Jesus" for our beloved, blue-eyed dad.

A few days before my father died, my husband and children flew in to say their final good-byes. I remember my dad asking Dan, "When will it be my turn to go?"

Dan looked at him lovingly and said, "Your time will come."

Then my dad whispered to Dan, "Eat more ice cream!"

With that, he forced his frail, thin arms into the air to wave at me across the room. Three times he pointed to himself and then to his heart and then toward me. With tears flowing down my cheeks, I mirrored back to him "I love you." He was never strong enough to lift his arms again. It was the last time he was able to tell me he loved me.

The hymn I sang during his last day was "Were You There?" Instead of singing "Were you there when they crucified my Lord?" I changed the words to "Were you there when the angels came for Paul? Were you there when they took him to the Lord?" I kissed my dad good-bye and told him I would take care of Mom and that he could go whenever he wanted to.

A few hours later, my brother called to tell us that my father had passed away. I rushed back to Kobacker House and held his warm hand for a few minutes before my mother and sister arrived. People from Schoedinger's Funeral Home came to speak with us and then rolled Dad out on a gurney to place him in the hearse. I hurried after them thinking, *This will be the last time I'll walk through a doorway with my dad, and I don't want to miss it.*

At the funeral, Dan, my brother, and my nephew John eulogized my father while I sat in the pew our family had occupied every Sunday of my childhood. I felt suddenly young again as childhood friends and friends of my parents surrounded me. In the midst of my grief, I found comfort in the beauty of this church and ballast in the hard pew. My traditional Methodist upbringing seemed fitting at such a sad time.

Following the funeral, we all gathered around the grave for a simple service. Shivering in the frigid winter chill, I lifted my gaze to the gray skies, thankful that the angels had taken my dad when he passed from this world to the next.

Everyone takes a final journey with their parents. This was my first. I am now an official member of the dead-parents society.

The Bible says that God is near to the brokenhearted (Psalm 34:18). He truly was and is near me. He is before me, beneath me, behind me, above me, and beside me. And I feel my father's presence all around me too. So often with the new technology available on my phone, I say to him, "Dad, you wouldn't believe this! Now I can send photos to you instantly!" Or "Dad, how did you make it around the world and across the country without Google Maps?" But most of all, I say things like "Dad, I miss you so much." And "My eyes still well up with tears when I think of you and remember our visits, vacations, and everyday life together."

Just this morning, I was at the dentist being fit for a new crown, and Cat Stevens came on over the office intercom. Instantly in my mind I could see Dad and me in his yellow Mazda with my Cat Stevens cassette playing "Peace Train," "Morning Has Broken," and "Father and Son." My heart was alive remembering how much we delighted in each other. I carry that priceless gift with me each day.

"I'll see you soon, Dad! Ten, twenty, thirty years ... I'm not sure when. But, hey, don't you think your grandchildren and great-grandchildren are amazing? You would love them so much, Dad! I tell them stories about you. You live in our hearts. I miss you more than ever, Dad. I love you."

QUESTIONS TO PONDER

Listen for echoes of your story in this essay and write about it in your journal. Then ponder the following questions and record your thoughts.

1. What do you fear most regarding a loved one's death?
2. How do regrets keep you from grieving?
3. What must you surrender to bless someone's departure?

Echoes of Gratitude

I had never heard something so loud on an airplane. It sounded like an explosion! I had never seen a more anguished look on my husband's face. What had happened? And what was about to happen? We had been looking forward to our Ireland bicycling trip with three other couples for quite some time. But it quickly faded from our minds.

The pilot eventually got on the intercom and said, "Folks, you might have noticed a loud boom at takeoff. Our tires exploded, and we're trying to decide if we should dump fuel and return to Denver, or if we should dump fuel on the way to O'Hare. I'll keep you informed."

A little while later, the pilot spoke again: "Folks, we've decided to proceed to Chicago."

I looked down at the sampler I was working on and couldn't believe the verse I was stitching: "In my Father's house are many mansions: if it were not so, I would have told you. I go to prepare a place for you. And if I go and prepare a place for you I will come again and receive you unto myself that where I am there ye may be also" (John 14:1–3, KJV).

The previous day, that Bible verse had seemed so comforting, but now, in this moment of such uncertainty, I felt near tears. I thought back over the past two days. My mother had called while we were packing and said that she'd had a dream of a plane crash. She even went so far as to say that maybe we should change one ticket so at least we weren't on the same aircraft.

Oddly, that same day Dan's personal assistant called to say she wanted to talk to him, and it sounded urgent. She came to our home and told Dan that she had a bad feeling about our trip. Did we really have to go?

Then that night Dan had a dream and saw a plane catch on fire after a heavy landing. It shook him so severely that he got out of bed, went to his study, and wrote a letter to each of our children in case something did happen. He placed the three letters in envelopes with their names on them and put them in his desk drawer without telling anyone. Nevertheless, we didn't heed the warnings. Everything was planned. Our sitters were in place, our bicycles were packed, and our plane tickets were paid for. We chose to go.

An hour before we were scheduled to land in Chicago, the pilot got on the intercom again and said that the flight attendants were going to pass out free drinks. As the carts quietly rolled down the aisle, solemn voices could be heard telling the attendants what they would like. Many people asked for more than one drink, and I wonder if that might have included me.

My breathing became harder as the magnitude of our plight sunk in. Was this to be the end? At one point Dan put his hands on my face and whispered, "Becky, you're hyperventilating, and you're really loud. You have got to breathe normally."

I didn't know how I was going to quit, but somehow, because of his touch, I quieted my breathing.

The time ticked on, and we said little. I married an articulate man who has used words not only as the tools of his occupation but also as a lifeline to save him from the complexity of his family of origin. He spoke to survive. But I could tell he was stumbling when he finally looked at me, his eyes filling with tears as he held my hands. "You have been the best wife any man could have ever had. Thank you."

How do you begin to express gratitude to a soul mate? How and what could I ever say to Dan to let him know how grateful I was for everything we had shared during our years together?

"Thank you for working so hard."

"Thank you for being so kind to our children."

"Thank you for getting us a dog."

As Dan and I looked into each other's eyes, the echo of gratitude continued.

"Thank you."

"No, thank you for thanking me."

"No, thank you for thanking me for thanking you."

It seems that the more grateful we are for someone, the harder it is to express what we feel. Our words seem too simple.

As we approached the airport, the flight attendants taught us how to assume the crash position; then the pilot told us to look out the window. There seemed to be a hundred bright-yellow emergency vehicles lining the runway. At the command, "Assume the brace position," Dan shoved me down with such force that my forehead scraped the seat in front of me, and my face ended up between my ankles. When we landed, we bounced up and then came down with a huge thud, and I could hear the fuselage scraping along the ground.

You would think everyone would have been cheering when the plane finally came to a stop, but it was eerily silent. When we got off the plane, I was shocked that no airline officials were there to offer consolation. At least after Dan and I had been stuck on a gondola in Vail, Colorado, we were given lunch vouchers! Nothing was spoken about the trauma we and the other passengers had just experienced. I really wanted to find a place to stand in the sunlight and pray. Dan, however, really wanted to get french fries and eat! Guess what? We got french fries and lots of ketchup and salt packets and laughed. It felt so good to be alive—and together.

I have many single friends who long to be married, and other friends who struggle daily in their relationships with men who don't own their fears, failures, or dreams. The last claim I'd make is that my marriage is easy. There have been lots of moments of agony as we've learned to become "one." There are many things we've had to die to. Nevertheless, while it isn't for me to ponder now, I can't imagine marrying again if Dan died. Some widows desire wholeheartedly to marry again, while others adapt to singleness and seem to thrive. It isn't for me to imagine what is not now, and by God's grace, it isn't something I'll need to ponder anytime soon. All I know is that if I find myself on my own death bed with Dan sitting next to me, I will say, "Thank you." And those words will echo in God's ear as I give Him all the glory for sustaining us through four decades of love.

Becky's handstitched Sampler

QUESTIONS TO PONDER

Listen for echoes of your story in this essay and write about it in your journal. Then ponder the following questions and record your thoughts.

1. Whom do you need to humbly thank, even if you stumble over your words?
2. What keeps you from expressing humble gratitude to those you love?
3. Think of a time when it was hard to receive someone's deep gratitude. How do you wish you would have responded?

Called to Remember

(F)all is my favorite season. The flowers begin fading, and I surrender to the end of summer while quietly embracing the need for routine. I welcome the return of a school schedule even though it is now the grandchildren who return to school, not me or my children. And it feels good, at least for now, that my husband returns to school as well.

Fall is also a time when I feel most melancholy as I notice the shortening of daylight and watch the dying leaves drop to the ground. I know that the Seattle rain and gray skies are coming soon. I appreciate the beauty of slanted rays of fall sunshine. I ground myself more rigorously in my morning yoga routine and begin purchasing candles that smell of autumn and home.

This week I took out the children's handmade Halloween crafts I chose to save. I carefully removed the orange paper jack-o'-lanterns and black paper bats and hung them from waxed string beneath our two chandeliers. In blue-and-gray crocks, I placed artificial bittersweet, which I purchased while my father was in hospice care. I put buckeyes from my great-uncle's home into a smooth wooden bowl in our foyer. Each year I do this in October and remember the weekend I returned home for my parents' fiftieth wedding-anniversary celebration on October 18th.

The leaves were brilliant and the sky was so blue that glorious fall weekend in Ohio. It was my first trip home without my children or husband. It was also the first time I had visited since my parents retired, and I wondered what our Monday or Tuesday would be like with them not rushing off to work.

Those five days at home were filled with a menagerie of emotions. I stayed with my brother because my aunt and uncle were staying at my parents' home. My brother's wife had recently left him, taking the kids with her. The house was tomb-like without his two-year-old son and four-year-old daughter. Every room echoed heartache, and I was gripped with sorrow even as I anticipated the anniversary celebration to come.

My brother, sister, and I honored my parents' wishes to have a small party at my sister's home. Many of the people who came had known my father since they were kids together in Grandview Heights, Ohio. I was near tears greeting people who had been part of my life from birth. *Why do I get so emotional?* I asked myself. *Why can't I be more even keeled like my brother and sister?* Instead, I felt the weight of the passage of time as it hit me that I might never see most of these people again.

On Monday morning, my father surprised my mother and me with a drive to Delaware, Ohio. He wouldn't tell us where we were going, but as we traveled, I realized that we were coming to my beloved Route 315, the road my dad and I had motorcycled on that wound along the Olentangy River. It was the road that led to Ohio Wesleyan University, as well as my grandparents' childhood homes.

When we arrived in Delaware, my dad drove up and down streets I had never been on before and stopped at a stately brick house I had never noticed before. We all got out of the car, and my mother and I followed Dad to the lawn, where he started picking up buckeyes and putting them in his pockets.

"Dad, what are you doing?" I asked.

He just kept on picking up buckeyes, far more than he could keep, so I started filling my coat pockets as well. Eventually he said that this was his great-uncle Jim's house. My parents' home contained furniture and crystal from Great Uncle Jim's house. It was sweet to stand on the lawn and put a house with the stories I had heard as a child.

Next my dad took us through the cemetery and showed us grave sites we had never visited before. Uncle Jim's grave marker was almost six feet tall! We walked up and down the rows as my dad told stories of his past. Then we drove by the church where my great-grandmother and her children had been allowed to live in the basement after her husband died. It felt sacred to see the actual church after only hearing about it from my grandfather. Why had we never done this before?

I felt both overwhelmed and grateful hearing my father tell stories about his family. So many new names, sights, and memories that seemed tossed into a basket like buckeyes. I never asked my father why he wanted me to encounter his past that day. I didn't understand then, but I have a better idea as I've aged. We want someone to witness our lives. We want our children, in particular, to help us manage the harvest of memories. We don't want to tend that fruit alone.

As I decorate for Halloween, I'm struck by how odd it is that I'm able to remember this holiday more clearly than others. The first Halloween Dan and I celebrated as newlyweds was a shocking eye opener. It was the fourth year of his master's of divinity studies in Philadelphia, and I had left him home alone to go to a quilting class. When I returned, I asked him if he had handed out all of the candy to the trick-or-treaters. He answered that he had given nothing away because he had studied the whole evening and never came down from the third-floor attic to answer the doorbell. I was horrified that I had married such a man! I made that clear, and he never missed the trick-or-treaters again.

Subsequent Halloweens brought varied weather and circumstances. We were poor while Dan worked on his three postgraduate degrees. I remember Dan taking Annie out on a blustery Michigan evening and can still see her wearing a flannel nightgown with the pink hand-stitched cape with a tin-foil-covered cardboard crown I had made. She looked darling. I stayed home passing out candy to the neighbors and was glad for the father-daughter time they were enjoying.

Two years later, in Indiana, Dan stayed home, lying by the door, to pass out the candy. He was awaiting back surgery. I pushed a stroller with toddler Amanda alongside seven-year-old Annie. The next year was the same: Dan lying by the front door, this time recovering from back surgery while I took our two daughters and infant son trick-or-treating.

As I prepare for Annie and her boys to come this Halloween weekend, Dan is participating in a fundraiser for the Anchor House in North Carolina, the very first residential shelter for sex-trafficked adolescent boys in our country. The shelter offers a refuge of hope, healing, and restoration from the abuse and exploitation they experienced in the sex trade.

Before my grandsons arrive, I take time to pray for these boys and so many like them in our country and around the world. I ache for those who have no place to lay their heads and whose lives have been ravaged by trafficking. Who will remember them? The prophet Isaiah, addressing a community of people in exile who believed that God had forgotten their desperate plight, penned these words:

Can a mother forget the baby at her breast
  and have no compassion on the child she has borne?
Though she may forget,
  I will not forget you!
See, I have engraved you on the palms of my hands;
  your walls are ever before me." (Isaiah 49:15–16)

God has carved our names into the palms of His hands! This is a profound reversal of expectation. In the ancient Near East, faithful followers of false gods would carve the names of their gods on their palms. Yahweh, in contrast, doesn't call us to do that. Instead, He cuts *our* names into *His* flesh. Like an eternal paper cut, He feels the agony of our exile and refuses to forget. He witnesses and records our tears, keeping them in a bottle until the day when all suffering will end.

I ache for violence against children to end. I want there to be no lack of beds for exploited children who need safety and healing. I want sex trafficking to end, and I want healing for those men who buy sex. I want awareness of trauma and effective treatment for it. I want this world to be swallowed up by a new heaven and a new earth. I'm so grateful to know there is a new day ahead when wrong will be righted, when sickness and sorrow will be no more. The new day my grandson loves to hear about when "the wolf will live with the lamb, the leopard will lie down with the goat, the calf and the lion and the yearling together" (Isaiah 11:6), when evil will no longer prowl endlessly on this earth. I believe in the resurrection of Jesus. I believe in the resurrection of the dead.

Nevertheless, as I read Scripture passages that give me hope to see the good, I will not forget the bad. When I pull out our Halloween decorations, I choose to enter my melancholy, which is about so much more than gray skies and wet cold. I no longer send my children trick-or-treating while I hand out candy to those fortunate enough to live protected from terrible harm; instead, I remember the children who may never get to take part in any holiday traditions.

As a child of God, I'm called to share with others the love and passion of my Father. I'm called to let melancholy enter and flow through me as I suffer with those who suffer. As I face the coming of winter, I choose to hear the cries of those who need rescuing. As I watch children dress up for Halloween, I choose to remember those who cannot. I choose to listen to stories of harm and be part of the healing process in any way I can. I am called to respond. I am called to remember.

QUESTIONS TO PONDER

Listen for echoes of your story in this essay and write about it in your journal. Then ponder the following questions and record your thoughts.

1. Do you intentionally set aside a time to tend to your memories? Why or why not?
2. What would it cost you to take time to remember a day or a specific event?
3. What would you gain if you spent time each day remembering the Lord your God?

Judge Not

After becoming involved with Late Night Outreach, I became a student of what I thought of as "street sociology." I was given a list of books to read and movies to watch and was challenged, in particular, to understand the trauma of the African American experience. My understanding had been slim without my realizing it. I often had to close a book or turn off a movie and breathe through the agony of what had been hidden from me about white privilege. I'm astounded at how little I was taught in American history courses!

I no longer look at my life the way I used to. I see what I have now as a privilege of my race. I've become aware of laws that have kept other races from having advantages I have taken for granted. The very neighborhood I grew up in had laws in the early sixties that banned blacks from purchasing houses or land there! I understand more clearly now how the Civil War didn't truly free slaves. New laws were put in place that ensured continued discrimination and made their "free" existence even more painful at times than their captivity.

If you weren't white, you had to work doubly hard and twice as long to get ahead. The great migration to the North was resisted with hate and oppression as well. The North wasn't going to accept blacks with any more enthusiasm than the white Southerners had. (So much for my false pride over not being from the South!)

This thought-provoking summary appeared in a web ad for Dr. Joy DeGruy's book *Post Traumatic Slave Syndrome*:

> Emancipation was followed by one hundred more years of institutionalized subjugation through the enactment of Black Codes and Jim Crow laws, peonage and convict leasing, and domestic terrorism and lynching.... What do repeated traumas visited upon generation after generation of a people produce?[2]

In my view, not a whole lot has changed. The mass incarceration of African Americans in our prison system is heartbreaking. The sometimes-brutal treatment of police toward African Americans is horrific. There continues to be race inequality all around us today. The importance of accepting all people as equals and loving without judging has never made more sense in my life.

This has been easier said than done for me as I faced some of the brutal realities on the streets. It has been especially difficult not to become jaded and angry with men. I have had the safety and love of a husband of forty years who appreciates and honors me, and I am much more aware of the gift and sanctity of being loved and cared for.

Still, it isn't easy to be a woman and not get caught in the crossfire of gender injustice. I've become embittered at times and prideful as a woman. I've experienced violence in my own heart in ways I didn't before. At one point I developed a cold stance toward males, including my husband. I'm sad about the anger that sometimes got directed at him. One way this leaked out was in a hardness and unwillingness to be sexual. To be more honest, I was repulsed by God's design for maleness and femaleness, and it took time to address my revulsion for sexual intimacy. I was arrogant. I was vigilant. I was harsh. I allowed the johns, the pimps, and the abused and broken women I met to sprawl out on our marriage bed.

By God's grace, my fury eventually gave way to sorrow, and I was able to redirect my anger toward the evil and brokenness in this world rather than toward the men who committed the crimes. I had to face my hatred of their cruelty and turn it into hatred of the evil that makes the sex trade possible. I believe that any judgment against men only adds to the darkness. Any disdain for any person or group only brings hardness and harm. I'm humbled to have love and not hate in my heart now because I know it isn't because of anything I've done. The kindness of God and the kindness of my husband changed my heart. If only the hearts of all people were open to one another and aware of their similarities more than their differences. Only love heals.

These days I find myself thinking of Jesus more and more. I see Him on the cross and can almost hear the voice of the thief hanging next to Him. I can see the guilty man as he turned toward our Savior and looked Him in the eyes, saying, "Remember me when you come into your kingdom" (Luke 23:42). I am that thief. I murder and steal in my thoughts. I need Jesus to "remember me." I'm so grateful for the grace that meets me wherever I am and reminds me that I need a savior as much as any man or woman I encountered on the street corner in the pouring rain.

It was freeing to go out to the streets of my city as an ambassador of love rather than a bearer of judgment. I could love the girls—and the men—and offer practical help without strings attached, without pressuring the girls to go in better directions, which they likely never would unless they knew they were worth loving. Once again I realized that I didn't have to be the change or the hope. God's Spirit did the heart-level work; I was simply His hands and feet, delighting in the girls and serving them hot chocolate, condoms, and hugs.

QUESTIONS TO PONDER

(L)isten for echoes of your story in this essay and write about it in your journal. Then ponder the following questions and record your thoughts.

1. White Americans seldom explore the depths of injustice our African American, Hispanic, Asian, Native American, or biracial friends suffer. What keeps you from exploring the stories of people who are racially different from you and naming the harm they've experienced?

2. Do you tend to make judgments about other people? What kinds of judgments do you make?

3. What do you think it would look like to live a day or a week without judging others?

A Miraculous Night

It was so cold outside that I couldn't imagine what I was going to wear. Record-breaking temperatures for our city were set three out of the past four days, and that night it wasn't expected to rise above twenty-two degrees. I pulled out my silk long underwear and my daughter's old ski pants, along with a polar-fleece pair of pants. I had six layers under my faithful black coat and carried three more layers in my backpack. I felt as if I were three years old and stuffed into a snowsuit that made me waddle. I tried not to think too far ahead. One moment at a time is the better way to approach a long, frigid night on the streets.

Everyone on our team arrived at the office at the same time, and we began the evening with prayers for the men and women we would be seeing later. I began filling thermoses with coffee and hot water, hoping they would get us through the night. Our home-baked treats were gingerbread blondies with white-chocolate chunks, wrapped in lovely packages and tied with red ribbon. Woodleigh brought whipped cream, crushed candy canes, and shaved chocolate for the hot chocolate. We made our little "stand" look festive and inviting.

Lori was the first to arrive for supplies and conversation. She was one of the friendliest women I knew. She had three sons—nine, six, and three years old—and was expecting her first daughter in March. We talked about her family, and she said that the boys' grandfather was taking them to look at Christmas lights that night. It was just what my father loved to do with me and my siblings. What does a father think when he takes his grandkids out to see the lights and knows that his daughter is standing on a shadowy corner as traffic lights illumine her half-naked body? Lori gave us hugs and declined hot drinks but filled a small purse with condoms before heading out into the night.

Harmony showed up in a short skirt with a sleeveless top that made us cringe. We were shivering, and I had five hand warmers in my boots and gloves! One of my teammates noticed that both of Harmony's heels were raw and bloody. She was so cold that she couldn't even feel her injuries. My coworker, Susan, asked her to sit on a cooler while she put on disposable gloves and plastered her heels with Band-Aids. Susan asked Harmony if she would like some Advil, but this young girl was numb to any pain. She didn't even want a hot drink. It was time to get back to the track and make her quota for the night, which might take seven hours.

As the night grew colder, I handed out a record number of hot ciders and hot chocolates. Nancy came for hot water at least ten times. How did she do it? Where did she go to the bathroom? I dared not drink one cup of anything for fear I'd have to use the restroom at the nearby motel. I would wait until the morning to hydrate!

For the past three hours, I had noticed a baby-blue Hummer driving through our intersection repeatedly. I looked at the man behind the wheel of this huge phallic machine and wondered if he thought he was incognito. The women called him Hummer Boy. The Jaguar had been there for hours too, as had the dented Toyota and the company heating-and-cooling van that circled for hours every Friday and Saturday night.

How hard would it be for police officers to report these cars? Why didn't they? Laws made by men one hundred or more years ago continue to drive me crazy! Let's get the johns and not our girls! Let's get the pimps who control the girls and not the girls! Or let's at least provide the girls a place for restoration, not punish them with a jail sentence. As I stood on the street watching the parade of lust, I wanted to scream. Once again I was finding it hard not to judge.

My heart was despairing as I served fifteen- and sixteen-year-olds hot chocolate and condoms. I wondered if this was where I should be. I used to feel more hope. But I saw more girls coming, and I was overwhelmed by the lack of impact our team seemed to have. I dared not say this to my coworkers. I felt as if I was betraying our mission. But at that moment, I couldn't imagine a couple more years of these nights.

Across the street I saw Barry and Don talking to some pimps. It was amazing to see all the men who stopped to talk now compared to six months earlier when we began our outreach. It bolstered my hope, and I found myself engaging our girls instead of pondering my despair. It wasn't up to me to change a single woman or man out there. So I served and prayed that these people (and myself) would be the recipients of love and mercy underserved but available because of His love. It wasn't normal for us to mix, yet there we stood, side by side, sharing tastes of kindness and civility. We were all recipients of grace in these odd encounters.

When it was time to pack up the van and head back to our headquarters, Barry and Don had great things to report. First of all, Vegas, a pimp usually on our streets, had called Don from Arizona to talk. They talked on their cell phones until Vegas's battery died. Don kept saying, "This was a miraculous night!" I was greatly encouraged by his enthusiasm.

Another one of the pimps had come by and said, "I'm coming to your house on Christmas! Is that all right?"

Don replied, "Of course, you come by!"

One pimp even said he'd gone to church on Sunday. I soaked all of this up. I'd had my most despairing night of the year, but our men were proclaiming the name of Jesus as healer and restorer and came away saying, "This was a miraculous night!"

I wondered how much this was like the first Christmas. A few were given a front-row seat to glory, but most people had no idea what was taking place. We can turn one way and see little but passing traffic, or turn another way and see powder-blue rage targeting an object on which to release its raw lust. Or we can turn and see a miracle taking place. It's all a matter of what we choose to see. That night I felt despair, while just feet from my frozen toes, my teammates were celebrating hope for transformation.

Back at our headquarters, we put away our supplies and said goodnight. I walked across the street and went up to my daughter and son-in-law's condo, tiptoeing in as quietly as one can with boots on. The couch was waiting for me with pillows and blankets, and I put all the hand warmers into my socks. What a fabulous feeling to lie down and know that I would be warm soon. I tried to think of every girl I'd met over the past year and said each name as a prayer. Eventually I drifted off to sleep knowing that, truly, it had been a miraculous night.

QUESTIONS TO PONDER

Listen for echoes of your story in this essay and write about it in your journal. Then ponder the following questions and record your thoughts.

1. Write about a time when someone else's joy transformed your discouragement.
2. God sometimes calls us to serve in strange places. When has the gospel called you to serve in a strange place?
3. Have you ever been clueless about how your behavior affected those around you? What finally made you aware of the harm you were causing?

Stranger or Angel?

Dan and I weren't sure what was best: try to outrun Hurricane Dennis in Florida or change our plans and arrive late in Lansing, Michigan, for his doctoral-program orientation. The plan was for Dan to drive our nineteen-foot U-Haul truck, with our Buick Monarch in tow, and for me to follow him in our manual-shift Volkswagen Rabbit, which I didn't know how to drive! Dan had me practice driving in a parking lot as rising water seeped through the floorboard. I could barely concentrate on the gears with the frightening water and wind that wouldn't let up. I could tell that this would be the fodder for nightmares yet to come.

We hadn't gone far before the U-Haul had engine trouble. We called the U-Haul headquarters, and a truck was sent to tow our truck to the mechanic's, because the idea of unloading everything was too much to bear. Eventually the truck was fixed, and Dan said, "Let's keep going!"

With shaking legs and arms and tears running down my cheeks, I got into the Volkswagen and locked my eyes on the Buick's taillights. It was crazy what we were doing, but it seemed equally crazy to stay where we were.

By nightfall we had gone as far as our bodies would tolerate. Thankfully, the hurricane had been downgraded to a tropical storm, but deep puddles were everywhere. Most of the motels had no vacancies, and our exhausted bodies were ready to give out. Since we were towing a car behind the U-Haul, we had to find a motel that had a turnaround. Finally, the fourth motel I checked had a room for us, and the late-night manager said yes, there was a turnaround.

Dan drove the truck into the cramped parking lot, and I followed in the Rabbit with eyes barely able to focus. Suddenly he slammed on the brakes, opened the truck door in a panic, and shouted, "We're doomed!" Not just once, but three more times he hollered our fate. Ahead, blocking the turnaround, was an area fenced off with two chain-link fences and a pile of dug-up concrete. Dan was right: We were doomed. The U-Haul and our Buick were stuck on a steep grade with no place to go.

If I thought I was shaky at the beginning of the trip, it was nothing compared to how I felt now with an enraged, scared husband. Although we had been married almost five years, I had never seen Dan so afraid. He sat down on the bumper of the car, covered his face, and wept. Then he asked me to go see if there was anyone in the motel who could come and help us.

As I walked toward the nearest door, I heard a voice behind me. When I looked back, I saw a short, muscular African American man walking toward Dan. I heard the man ask Dan what was wrong, and Dan explained that there was no way he could back out of the driveway with our car on the hitch behind the U-Haul truck. The man answered, "Let's try to get it off."

They went over to the truck, and the man instructed Dan to unhook the latch holding the U-Haul frame on the towing ball. Then they each took a separate side and pulled the car off the ball. Dan later told me that as he pulled with all his might, he could tell he wasn't moving the car an inch; however, the other man seemed to lift the car without effort.

After the car was unhooked, Dan pulled the truck away, and the man told me to get into the car and put it in neutral so they could turn it downhill and reconnect it to the truck. It seemed impossible in that tight space, but as they pushed and I steered, eventually the car ended up pointing in the right direction, and Dan and the man lifted it back onto the hitch.

After a huge sigh of relief, Dan said, "Let me give you some money to thank you for your help."

But the man shook his head and said, "No, all I ask is that you do something good for someone else."

I ran to get my wallet so I could give him a twenty-dollar bill anyway, but he disappeared. Our backs had been turned less than twenty seconds! There was no way he could have gotten through or over the two chain-link fences that fast, and yet the man was gone.

Dan and I looked at each other with wide eyes. Then he whispered, "I think that man was an angel."

It was so holy and so outrageous a thought that we said nothing more about it for many years. Truly, it was a story that took years to tell.

"**D**o not forget to show hospitality to strangers," the apostle Paul told the Hebrews, "for by so doing some people have shown hospitality to angels without knowing it" (Hebrews 13:2). Dan and I sometimes read Bible stories about angels to our children but didn't tell them that angels are real and active. Now that I'm a grandmother, things have changed. I've found it so sweet to call forth angels to come to our aid, and I assure our grandchildren that they each have their own angel watching over them.

Cole is eight years old, our oldest grandchild. He is sensitive and thoughtful like his mother, Annie. He even looks like her and has that big-boy serious side that lots of firstborn children come equipped with. He is old enough to appreciate the holiness of God sending help to a couple in need.

Dan and I have great power to speak truth to our grandchildren, and I want to steward this opportunity with grace. When we read Scripture with them in their children's Bibles, the pages that depict angels are often the ones where we to linger the longest. One drawing of the angel appearing to the shepherds to proclaim the good news of a babe born in Bethlehem spreads across two full pages. I love how we have to turn the book sideways to see the magnitude of the glory that leveled the shepherds on the ground, their fearful faces in the dirt. Much of life as I age seems to have me facedown and calling on an angel!

When my father was dying, I heard a voice remind me that God's grace was sufficient for that trial. I was new at this "hearing God" thing and was calmed when I sensed Him whispering to my heart, "My timing is perfect." When my mind would race ahead to all the unknowns of this experience, I would hear again, "My grace is sufficient. My timing is perfect." It was as though God had sent an angel to sit on my shoulder and give me strength for each moment as it unfolded.

The same has been true throughout my life. The Bible says that the Word spoke the world into existence (Genesis 1; John 1:1–3). The words of God, angels, and men and women have power. I believe that the spoken word, my spoken word, can shine light or create darkness. The angel who helped move our car off the trailer hitch spoke words that shed light on our path. To this day, Dan and I call his help a miracle.

So was it just a good Samaritan who helped us that night so many years ago? I don't know for sure; I can't prove or disprove that a mere man can disappear in less than twenty seconds. But I've learned to take a closer look at the stranger who extends a strong hand and ponder, "Oh terrifying friend, where do you really come from?" And "Who are you asking me to be?"

QUESTIONS TO PONDER

Listen for echoes of your story in this essay and write about it in your journal. Then ponder the following questions and record your thoughts.

1. Have you ever thought you might have encountered an angel? What impact did this experience have on your life?

2. How might your view of life change if you realized that the unseen world around you is far more active than you believe it is?

3. If angelic encounters are possible in this life, does this change your view of hospitality? In what way?

You *Can* Go Home Again

Thomas Wolfe wrote a novel titled *You Can't Go Home Again.* Actually, you can.

It was time for our forty-fifth high school reunion, and as usual, I had to encourage my husband to go. "It's a good time to combine seeing family and friends," I said. But, as always, it took some convincing.

Dan and I went to the same high school but had completely different experiences. For me, high school was like a magic carpet whisking me away from the turmoil at home. Dan had already escaped his family by spending most of his time at his friend Tremper's house.

Dan's father owned a bakery and was rarely at home, and his mother desperately—and inappropriately—clamored for Dan's love and care. His mother was a substitute teacher, and her only friend was the neighbor across the street. When Dan's father saw the growing bond between his son and his fragile wife, he insisted that Dan go away to summer camp. The camp turned out to be a place of torture, where the counselors and older campers subjected him to bullying and sexual abuse. This horrific experience made him ready for a fight with anyone. He wasn't a bully who targeted the weak, but he made sure he was known as a tough guy who shouldn't be crossed. Playing football at school was Dan's ticket to freedom and a channel for venting his anger over the abuse he experienced and his parents' cluelessness.

Our high school's tradition is to hold a class reunion every five years on the Fourth of July. I'm always eager to reconnect with my friends, and Dan, because he loves me, comes with me even though it's the last place he wants to be. It may sound too severe, but I also go back for the same reason veterans return to be with their comrades long after the war is over. Veterans need to be reminded that life wins; death doesn't have the final word.

While high school was easier for me than it was for my husband, it was also a war zone. The wounds and scars of adolescence are usually hidden for at least twenty years afterward. It seems we need to be decades away from the turmoil to begin processing all that we suffered. The popular girls weren't that confident after all. The jocks were wondering if they had already hit their peak. The tech geeks didn't realize they would one day rule the world. None of us had a clue what was ahead. But the future opened before us like a Montana sky—vast, beautiful, and ominous.

I'm convinced that the best way to lean into the future is to bless and honor the gifts of the past. When I'm with friend Paula from elementary school, I remember the young Becky in second grade who moved to a new neighborhood. I remember Paula's kindness and her tenderly holding my new puppy, Pixie. I remember Paula's parents, her home, and her mother and mine being leaders of our Bluebird troop in Paula's basement. I remember transferring to my new elementary school after Easter weekend. I remember being scared to death riding in my father's Volkswagen to the parking lot and being escorted to Miss Myers's second-grade class. I remember Sara Smith being assigned to me for the week to see that I got to all the places I needed to go. I remember the smell of the cafeteria; Dessy, the overweight, beautiful cook with silver braids that wrapped around the crown of her head; and Kirby, the rotund, gray-haired custodian who always greeted me and made sure everyone had a four-cent milk carton at lunch. I loved elementary school.

Junior high became sketchier for me, with traumatic memories of cotillion dinner dances; algebra; biology; study halls; the large, looming cafeteria; and no recesses. A few times I got off the school bus before my stop and walked to my elementary school to visit my fifth- and sixth-grade teachers. I longed to be back at Windermere, where life seemed simpler and kinder. Hastings, with its lockers and classroom changes each period, made life feel less secure and more uncertain.

After three years, my friends and I couldn't wait to leave junior high. High school ushered in football games, school musicals, report cards, finals, boyfriends, school dances, and driver's licenses. During our senior year, the dress code changed, and we could wear pants to school. Alongside pants, miniskirts, and marijuana, our rage against the Vietnam War grew fierce, and our world seemed crazier with the assassinations of John F. Kennedy, Bobby Kennedy, and Martin Luther King Jr. We had lived through the Cold War, the Cuban missile crisis, the Bay of Pigs, and four students killed on the Kent State University campus not far away. Life seemed to be spinning out of control, and by the time we graduated, we were ready to leave. As soon as we could, we scattered with the wind.

Yet our class and our friends have stayed connected. Cliques have faded, and friendships have moved past lines that once were rigid. At this stage of life, there is little boasting. Careers, accomplishments, and wealth aren't entities that separate us. We've lost forty classmates, and many are currently fighting life-threatening illnesses. We've weathered losing parents, children, siblings, and marriages. We have become a class where "class" doesn't matter. When I see my friends from the class of '70, I see the spirit of Barb or the spirit of Linda. They aren't senior citizens to me; they're kids I knew at a younger time in my life.

To return to a class reunion isn't the same for Dan. He's a different man from the angry, scary, all-state football player who had a reputation that separated and protected him from his peers. Since then, the love of Jesus changed his heart and set him free. His decades of helping those who have been harmed by sexual violence have broken his heart open, and he is now a very kind and tender man. His bad-boy persona is gone—well, perhaps not entirely. Given all of this history, going back to his high school reunion brings up a painful past. It brings to mind that young Dan who suffered and caused suffering. He would have been thrilled to skip the whole experience.

When we arrived at the Barn at Hayden Falls, it was dim and cool inside, and our eyes had to adjust to the dark. The music of the late sixties was blaring, and the Beatles song "Here Comes the Sun" brought joy to my heart. Friends immediately swept me away, and I lost sight of Dan.

As it turned out, a man came up to him and spoke boldly: "I remember you, Dan Allender!" Dan didn't remember him, but the man certainly remembered Dan. "You used to scare me by your intimidating presence. I feared what you might do to me and avoided you at all costs, except in English class, where you sat behind me. It was miserable to fear you all year long our junior year. But I listened to your podcast about returning to this class reunion, and, holy cow, you've changed! I can tell that knowing Christ has softened you. It's amazing to stand with you and no longer fear you. I would like to hear more about how you've changed since you sat behind me all those years ago."

Dan sought me out after that interaction. His face was joyful as he said, "That conversation alone was worth the trip."

Every day a glance at the news leaves me feeling like death will win and the meek won't inherit the earth but will instead be lost in the trash heap of history. Power, violence, and arrogance win elections and propel people to the top of the food chain no matter the field or endeavor. I'm grateful that God gives me hints, small tokens from another realm to remind me that the human heart can change, and truth can replace lies and fear. I need to remember who I am, where I came from, and where I'm headed. It is this deep connection to my true destiny along with strong sinews of friendship that allow me to see that death is inevitable, but it never has the final word.

QUESTIONS TO PONDER

Listen for echoes of your story in this essay and write about it in your journal. Then ponder the following questions and record your thoughts.

1. How do you think the high school friends who haven't been part of your adult life might describe you?
2. What would surprise them most about the person you have become?
3. What would you expect and desire if you decided to attend your next high school reunion?

Requiem

I just addressed a pink envelope and put in a birthday card with pink cherry blossoms to mail to my friend Jane. She loves pink, she loves her family, she loves her friends, and I love her.

The first time I noticed Jane, we were sophomores in high school. She was swearing like a sailor in the kindest voice while eating peanut M&M's with a friend. I was intrigued because the only swearing I had heard was when my parents were angry.

We ended up sitting near each other in senior English class and became fast friends. In the spring, before a pop quiz, I asked her if she wanted to be roommates in college. I knew she planned to live at home, but I asked her anyway. It remains one of the best questions I've ever asked. She said yes.

We went off to college in 1970, leaving behind our suburban naïveté and exchanging it for young-adult realities. Panty raids gave way to SDS riots (Students for a Democratic Society), and women's rights and race riots brought conversations neither of us had ever had before. We were catapulted into experiences we wanted, and some we didn't. One thing never changed, and that was our care for each other.

Before our junior year, I transferred to a university out west, and Jane and I wrote often. Since then we've never lived near each other, but wherever I've lived and made new friends, they have known about Jane. She visited Dan and I at our cabana hut in Florida, an attic in Pennsylvania, then back to two houses in Florida, a garage in Michigan, two houses in Indiana, two houses in Colorado and our current house in Washington State. She and her partner, Bob, also attended each of our children's weddings.

In the rush at one daughter's wedding in Sayulita, Mexico, Dan and I were only able to enjoy breakfast with Jane and Bob while they waited for their ride to the airport. We laughed as Bob described his attempts to balance on a surfboard for the first time the previous day.

He was so full of life! When the driver arrived, I jumped up and had Dan take my photo with Jane. But since I have an annoying habit of taking too many pictures, I didn't snap one of Jane and Bob together. Oh, how I wish I had!

Later that day, as Dan and I were on our way back to Bainbridge Island, I received a call from Jane to say that Bob wasn't feeling well, and she was getting some medicine for him before they drove home.

When we got home, my cell phone dinged. It was a text from Jane. "Pray," it said. "Bob has chest pains. Driving to the hospital."

Reality got too real too fast. I wanted to call her, but I knew this wasn't the time. I was the out-of-town friend, and Jane's sister, Kathy, or her friend Amy or Mary Ann would be rushing to the hospital to be with her. I texted back "Praying."

I began unpacking and walked from room to room with my phone in hand. An hour later, another ding: "Torn aorta. In surgery." My heart thumped, and I ran to find Dan. Stunned by the news of what Jane and Bob were enduring, we stopped, sat, and prayed. Time stood still even though the clock hands moved.

Thirty minutes later, ding: "Arrested during surgery. Keep praying."

What? Did *arrested* mean what I thought it meant? This couldn't be happening! Once again Dan and I prayed. Nothing was more important than that. Who cared about laundry?

Four hours later I got a call from Jane. But it wasn't Jane; it was Mary Ann, her best friend since kindergarten, using Jane's cell phone. "She says she'll fall apart if she hears your voice, so I'm calling for her. Becky, the surgeon just left the family waiting room. It's bad. It's really bad. I'm going to spend the night with her after we see Bob in recovery in two more hours. It will be a long road."

B ob's life bobbed up and down like a lifesaver in tumultuous seas. Jane called that evening. Her voice sounded tired, and I could tell she was in shock but being strong because the story was far from over. Our calls over the next few days were hallowed as I rushed to my closet, knowing it was the best place to talk and not be disturbed. I hung on every word as Jane recounted the day, conversations with physicians, and Bob's beautiful, blank blue eyes staring back at her.

"Becky, I don't think he's in there."

Some evenings Jane began the call by saying, "Talk to me about your day. Talk to me about something normal." And I did, even though I didn't want to. I told her about shopping with our four-year-old grandson, and how he pulled the pickle jar off the grocery shelf. I told her about Amanda's honeymoon fiasco.

One evening we laughed and laughed and laughed some more. "Thank you, Beck," she said. "I needed that."

Downstairs my family waited to hear how Bob was, how Jane was. How could I tell them we had laughed together for almost half an hour? I wish I could remember what made us laugh. Was it an odd story of Jane's or mine? No clue. But I was the friend she could let down with in the safety of her bed at night after a full day and evening at the hospital.

One morning, hope was back after the surgeon called Jane at her home. "He needs more time," the doctor said.

Could we hope for a miracle because hundreds of people were praying? Was this the time when limbs would move and eyes would see and recovery would truly begin? The surgeon was a man of hope. He was the talk of the floor, Jane said. He was young. He was amazing. Jane really liked him. He was the beacon that lured her to believe that Bob could recover.

"I've seen people come out of states like this," he said. "Bob needs more time. We must give him more time."

The evening phone calls with Jane remained holy, and her friend Amy became my point person to call during the day to find out how Bob and Jane were doing. I kept asking Jane when she wanted me to come. She kept saying, "Not yet." And then, after a few days and consultations with the neurologist and surgeon, everything changed and hospice was called in.

I wanted to scream. I fell to the floor and pounded the carpet and moaned, "No! I can't bear this for my friend. I love Bob too! I hate this, God! Please, no!" Yet it isn't what I think of God and what He is doing, but rather, what God thinks of me and Jane and Bob and all of us.

"Take this cup away," I prayed, "but if You don't, Your will be done."

Although it felt as if we were free-falling through the darkness, we weren't alone. Jane's next text had a different tone: "Holding Bob's hand in a sunny room. There is no other place I want to be. I am at peace with my Bob."

Friends came to stand by Bob's bed and say their good-byes. Some people said they wanted to remember Bob alive and wouldn't come, while others stood quiet vigil. Some came to thank Bob for everything he had done for them. The ambulance came and took him to the hospice facility, and Jane was driven home to pack her suitcase and spend her final nights with Bob. The two nights Jane was there, the nurse helped tuck her in next to the love of her life.

Bob died at 1:00 a.m., and it was Jane who noticed and then consoled the nurse when his death was confirmed. She texted me the next morning, and I knew it was time to go.

Our days together were simple, and there was a rhythm of sorrow and laughter and remembrance. We stayed up late talking about Bob. We got up early and talked about the arrangements for his memorial service. Jane's sister, Kathy, and her husband, Frank, came over. Mary Jo, whom I hadn't seen in nearly thirty years, came from Cleveland with handmade Italian cookies and cakes. We helped each other decide what we would wear to the service. It was all real and surreal at the same time.

On the morning I flew home, Jane and I got up at three o'clock. Jane brewed coffee, and we sipped its soothing warmth into our bodies at her kitchen table before she drove me to Port Columbus International Airport. We'd spent a lifetime going to that airport together. We backpacked in Europe together after college, and our families sent us off and greeted us when we returned. When my father could no longer pick me up at the airport, Jane would be waiting for me curbside when I arrived to visit my mother.

And when my mother died, Jane and Bob picked up my husband at the airport and got him to the funeral just in time. Jane and I had hugged and held each other. She surprised me with a care package filled with food that friends had brought—friends who needed to bring food to ease their own grief.

The Eucharist I had savored on my way home was the chocolate-peanut-butter Clif Bar that should have been eaten on Bob and Jane's trip home from Mexico. Each bite I took felt like betraying a dream. But now my dream shifted from wishing Jane and Bob a safe trip to blessing the bounty of Bob's eternity.

We are each a passing presence, a breath with flesh and dreams. One breath we are here, and the next we become the tears of the living and the laughter of heaven. How do we bear the suddenness and cruelty of death and not lose the delight and sweetness of life? It isn't by merely vowing to live each day to the fullest. Each day is already full. Bearing the cruelty of death is a weight that friends are meant to carry together. We are to help each other drink the cup of sorrow and taste the sweetness of resurrection. It is our meal, our chocolate-peanut-butter Clif Bar.

Fair winds and blue skies, Bob.

Bob and Jane

QUESTIONS TO PONDER

Listen for echoes of your story in this essay and write about it in your journal. Then ponder the following questions and record your thoughts.

1. Whom would you drop everything to be with if he or she experienced a devastating loss? What are the stories that bind your heart to that person?
2. In what ways do the dead remind you of how you want to live?
3. Does the fear of saying the wrong thing or causing pain keep you from talking with someone about a loved one he or she lost? What actions might offer comfort when you're at a loss for words?

Second Chances

I was relieved that the first set of visiting hours at the funeral home had gone well, whatever that meant! What is "well" at your mother's viewing? Is it the number of people who come? Is it their words describing what your mother meant to them? Is it the unexpected childhood friends who drive long distances to say, "I am so sorry for your loss"? Death is surreal.

My husband and I had spent the previous nine months traveling abroad, and this was to have been the end of our sabbatical: a visit with my mother over Mother's Day. Well, not Dan, but me. This was to have been my first Mother's Day with my mother since college. Instead, we would be burying her next to my father the day before Mother's Day. Life is surreal.

When the afternoon visiting hours were over, my sister and brother and I drove to our childhood home in silence and ate our first meal at the dining-room table for the first time without my mother. All I remember before returning to the funeral home for the evening viewing was eating the chocolate-chip cookies Beulah had made. Beulah, who was the mother of my long-time childhood friend Julie, had always been like a second mom to me, and her cookies softened my grief.

The after-work crowd that showed up for the viewing turned the affair into a mini-high-school reunion of Upper Arlington classes of 1967, 1970, and 1976. It was a comfort talking with old friends from various clubs my mother had been involved in, as well as neighbors and church members who had watched me grow up. The conversation I had with Julie, however, took me by surprise.

"Your mom was so proud of you," she said.

"No, she wasn't," I rebutted.

"She would come home from visiting you and tell everyone about your home, your children, and you."

"No, she didn't."

"Yes, she did. I was there with my parents and their friends. She couldn't wait to give us the latest description of whatever state you had moved to and how you were doing."

"I can't believe you're saying this, Julie. I never heard anything close to what you're telling me. I longed for her approval. I longed for her affirmation about anything. Anything! But according to her, I didn't discipline my children correctly, my hair was never styled like she wanted, my clothing was never up to her standard. Even your mother told me not to try to please her because I would never be able to. Why are you telling me this now? You know my mom … knew my mom, I mean."

We stared at each other, and I finally said, "Why didn't she tell *me* those things?"

I awkwardly turned to the next person, and soon it was time to load up the car with items we had brought to represent Mom's life. My mother's sport was shopping, and a Talbots shopping bag made everyone smile. I was always proud of the way she dressed.

The following day, Dan arrived to eulogize my mother, along with my brother, nephew, and the Methodist minister who had walked alongside us over the past few days. We brought sailing trophies, oil paintings, her Bible, and a few aprons because she was a fabulous cook and loved to entertain. Soon after the memorial service, Dan returned to Bainbridge Island, my sister and her husband left for their Canadian vacation, and my brother and his wife flew to China. My friend Julie left for Florida, and Jane went to Lake Erie. I was alone.

I headed over to my parents' empty house, unlocked the back door and stepped into the kitchen. The silence enveloped me, and I slid to the floor, wrapping my arms around my knees. *What do I do now? Where do I start? Do I begin emptying the refrigerator? Do I go up to my old bedroom and unpack my suitcase?*

I decided to carry my suitcase upstairs, where I began opening windows. The smell of summer wafted into my bedroom. Oh, I hadn't smelled the English privet hedge so strongly since the fifth grade, before air-conditioning was installed.

Then I went into my parents' bedroom. I touched the bed, sat in the rocking chair, opened their closet doors—looking for what, I'm not sure. There on my mother's closet shelf was a diary. *What?* I grabbed it and ran back to my twin bed, where I devoured every page. I learned things I never knew and some I never wanted to know, but even in the darkest entries, I felt like I got a second chance to know my inscrutable mother. For the first time I felt I had been invited into her scarred heart and could walk with her through some of her trauma.

I learned a few things in the first quick reading: My mother had wanted to back out of her own wedding because she had loved another man—an air-force pilot—during the war. The night before the wedding, her mother asked a Baptist minister to speak with her as the hours clicked by. I was shocked reading this, but it helped me see my mother as a real person. I, too, had doubts about marrying my husband and had called off our engagement because I wasn't sure that marriage was right for us. Knowing that my mother and I had this in common deepened my empathy for her.

Last photo with mom

Another shock was reading about the other men my mom dated during the war years when she was a young, unsupervised woman in Glendale, California. There were so many accounts of steak dinners and staying out until two o'clock in the morning! I also found it odd that she was so wrapped up in her own life that she never once reflected on the war in her writings. Not once did she mention the politics, the battles, or the news-flash short films that were shown before every movie in the theater. But even that was an insight into her frailty.

After reading my mother's diary, I wished she had sought more healing for the wounds she covered up with religious rigidity and social protocols. I wished counseling had been an accepted and respected option of care. I wished the pain of losing her dad could have been talked though so she could have grieved as a child. I've learned that when we grieve, we must return to the first grief we experienced before we can grieve the current loss. After my dad died, my mom began sharing with her friend Phyllis about what it was like to lose her father when she was fourteen. Phyllis would call me and say, "Becky, I never knew how her dad's death had left her so brokenhearted."

The more I began to know my mother after we buried her, the larger my heart toward her grew. My second chance at knowing her is one of the reasons I began to write. My children fiercely love me. My grandchildren delight to be with their Mia. But as it is with most children and grandchildren, the questions they will want to ask of me won't come to them until I am likely to be missing my mind or have left this earth. Everyone deserves a second and a third and endless chances to know those they knew only in part but long to know in full.

I don't know why my mother placed her secret journal in such an obvious place, but I choose to believe that she wanted her children to know something about her hidden heart. The diary answered some of the tens of hundreds of questions I had about why she behaved the way she did, and each answer was a tender ache that made me anticipate the day when we are fully reconciled.

QUESTIONS TO PONDER

Listen for echoes of your story in this essay and write about it in your journal. Then ponder the following questions and record your thoughts.

1. Do you plan to share the stories that shaped you with your children, family, and friends? Why or why not?

2. Read *The War of Art* by Steven Pressfield and reflect on the obstacles he discusses. What is keeping you from creating this gift of life stories for those you love?

3. It takes only five minutes to write a handful of sentences. What would you have to give up to write for five minutes each day?

Happy Back-to-School Day!

Most people say that being a grandparent is better than being a parent. Less responsibility. Less energy expended. More wisdom and another chance to get it "right." (There is actually no such thing, by the way.) And then, of course, there is the relief of sending our grandchildren back to their parents at the end of the day!

I do love being a grandmother, with all its simpler joys. I cherish every moment I spend with my grandchildren, and yes, I'm happy that I get to send them back to their parents! But I just don't buy the line that being a grandparent is better than being a parent. At least not for me. Maybe it is more fun at times to be a grandmother, but I still love being a mom.

I read a wonderful blog on Facebook today by Kim Simon.[3] Tears flowed down my cheeks before I knew it. Each sentence Kim had crafted took me back to the wonder of the brand new world that unveils itself to a mother. The author pondered, "How did we get here?" And then she brilliantly expounded on many of the things we did to get to the point of launching a kindergartner. As moms and moms-to-be, we experienced so many firsts: trying to get pregnant, staying pregnant, giving birth, cutting off the hospital bracelet, marveling when our babies walked for the first time and cut their first teeth.

Becky and her three children

As I read Kim's blog, I couldn't help but think about the many firsts that came with mothering my own young children: celebrating their first birthdays, delighting in their first words, attending their preschool graduations. I vividly remember weaning each of my children. I loved being a nursing mom. It was so maternal, so Mother Earth radical after my mother's bottle-feeding generation. My father photographed me reading *The Womanly Art of Breastfeeding* as I sat on the couch in our Florida home helping Annie unhinge her tongue from the roof of her mouth. It was a feminine sumo-wrestling act of love, and I embraced it with wonder and passion.

I nursed my other two babies, too. Only a few times I wondered with annoyance when I would ever be able to wear a silk dress to church again. When would this season of leaking on a blouse or wearing loose-fitting tops end? But honestly, I usually reveled in the miracle of feeding my babies with my own milk. I would ponder how hard the last time to nurse them would be. Tears would come to my eyes at the thought of the end of this phase.

Almost twenty years later, I sat in the passenger seat as Annie, a senior in high school, drove to the metro park tennis courts in the black Volkswagen Jetta she had bought with babysitting money. She hoped to make it to state finals again. If she won this match, it would happen. I still remember the intensity of the match. It was close, but from the start it appeared that the other player was just a bit better. Every time Annie fought back to tie the score, the other player nudged ahead. The match ended 6–4, 6–4.

I watched Annie shake hands with her opponent and graciously congratulate her for a match well played. Afterward, we walked silently to the car, and I wasn't sure if I should speak. Before she turned on the ignition, she turned to me and commented, "I just didn't want it to end." We looked at each other, and our eyes said it all: This was the end of an era. There would be no tennis team in college. My daughter's sports career was over.

The words Annie spoke seared my heart. The firstborn ushers us into the endings of so many things, so we are a bit more prepared as parents with our younger ones, but I never welcomed the inevitable endings involved in the adventure of raising my children.

At some point, we moms will look back and wonder how we did it. How did we help our kids through not being invited to birthday parties without letting them know that we were more hurt and angry than they were? How did we learn to accept our child when he wasn't in the highest reading group? How did we encourage our child when an injury kept her from playing basketball during her final season? How did we bear both the joy and the heartache that come with young love?

I think we did it by becoming detectives of our children and boldly entering their worlds, even when it was hard. We learned to study them carefully to see what made them unique. We found places, classes, or activities that fostered their minds and bodies. We learned not to compare our children to others, especially their siblings. We watched our children lose friends for insignificant reasons, and we saw them befriend others and start over again. We empathized when our daughters didn't get asked to dances, and our sons were a foot shorter than their seventh-grade dates. We agonized over our kids being too bright and not fitting in, and we worried about them not getting high SAT scores.

Our hearts ached when our children weren't accepted to their first choice of college or when we had to say no to the college they wanted because we couldn't afford it. We weathered their homesickness in college and unhappiness that required transfers. We agonized over first jobs that weren't good fits and boyfriends who didn't want to get engaged. We loved their fiancés and learned to let go so our children could create their own families. We relived our own pregnancies through theirs, and we couldn't believe how intensely we loved our newborn grandchildren. We babysat and merged with in-laws and spent holidays alone and got criticized for our shortcomings as parents. We thought of our deceased parents and wished we could tell them how much we realized now all that they did for us.

So, is it better to be a grandparent? It's fun, for sure, and it's true that there is less responsibility. But youth has a beauty, passion, and vitality that I miss. Sometimes I long to walk beside my children the same way I did when they were young. But would I do it over again? Would I want to return to being thirty-two and sending my firstborn off to kindergarten? Nope. I'm closer to heaven than ever before, and I wouldn't go back and relive all that I loved and all that broke my heart. My children wouldn't want to either. But I'm just as passionate as ever about giving my adult children the mothering that most of us yearn for throughout our days. We never get too old to need a mom, to need love and encouragement and validation. I see you! I see how hard you strive to be all you are for your family and your work and your calling.

So I will be content with not being one of those young mothers reading the blog today. I will ponder the joys and sorrows that have been my journey and be grateful for the countless blessings and hard knocks that have been my lot and my life. I will continue to embrace being a grandmother. But first and foremost, I will celebrate being a mom.

Happy back-to-school day to the young and the old! Happy back-to-school day to those who remember their own beginnings and find themselves amazed at the territory they have traversed. Happy back-to-school day to each mother and grandmother who wonders, *How did I get here?*—sometimes with tears streaming down her cheeks.

The Allender family together

QUESTIONS TO PONDER

Listen for echoes of your story in this essay and write about it in your journal. Then ponder the following questions and record your thoughts.

1. What is your sweetest memory of being a mother, whether or not you have children?
2. Who has been the best mother in your life?
3. Write about a golden moment with your mother that you'll always cherish.

Paying It Forward

My son and daughter-in-law needed a break. And I needed time with my granddaughter, since Dan was on the road. Sometimes needs dovetail so beautifully.

While I waited for Andrew and Elizabeth to bring over Elsa, I thought back to the times my parents would drop off my older sister and me at my grandparents' house on Wyandotte Road in Grandview Heights, Ohio. In the front yard was the "Becky tree," and in the backyard was the "Judy tree." My grandmother would often make applesauce with the apples from the Judy tree. We would help pick the apples while standing on metal chairs that rocked while my grandfather stood nearby in case we lost our balance.

On a hot summer day, we would sometimes sit on the wicker chairs on the front porch and listen to the leaves gently blowing. There was a swing set in their backyard, and they would push us for hours, or so it seemed. If we were good, we got to walk in our seersucker shorts and matching midriff tops to the corner drugstore to buy a lime or root-beer popsicle.

In the winter I would lie down near the grates in the dark wood floor when the furnace came on and call Pepper, their small, short-haired dog, to lie down next to me. I'd pass the hours petting his shiny coat and feeling his soft back rise and fall. The pace of life was so much slower than at our house, and no one ever asked me to do anything.

My grandparents' bedroom was downstairs, and ours was upstairs. There was no heat upstairs in their 1922 Craftsman house, so my grandmother gave my sister and me hot-water bottles to sleep with to help us stay warm. At bedtime she would walk us up the dark walnut stairs, and after we had said our prayers, she would always add, "Nighty-night, and don't let the bedbugs bite" before she turned off the light. During the day, both my grandparents would sit and talk to us. I felt seen and heard, and nothing felt urgent.

I have a picture of my last birthday dinner celebration at their home when I turned six. I guess I was allowed to carry my own cake into the dining room with the candles lit (with Grandma beside me) while everyone sang "Happy Birthday."

Becky's last birthday on Wyandotte Road

A few months later, my grandparents moved to Saint Petersburg, Florida. I wrote to them every month, and my grandmother wrote me back. She always signed every letter, "Oceans of love, Grandma and Granddaddy."

D an and I lived in Boca Raton, Florida, after we married, and we would make harrowing trips in our little lime-green MG Midget across Alligator Alley in torrential rainstorms to spend a weekend with my grandparents. It was wonderful to have Dan get a glimpse of who they were and how much I loved them. The day my grandfather died, I got permission to leave my teaching job for two days and drive over to be with Grandma, since I was the only relative in Florida. I felt so inadequate to ease her sorrow. Two years later when she died, I sat hugging my firstborn toddler with an ache that actually hurt. It still hurts these many years later when I allow myself to miss the goodness their lives brought to mine.

During the course of my childhood, I actually spent very few days with my grandparents. I would visit them on family vacations, but those trips were few and far between. And yet deep imprints of love were grooved into my heart and mind. Being with my grandparents had an impact on me that has lasted a lifetime. Those memories are a refuge in a world that feels progressively harder and scarier. I use them like withdrawals from a bank account that never runs out.

Now I have five grandchildren of my own. I see them often, and even if I didn't, I believe that my love for them would mark their lives in rich ways, some of which I will never see.

While I waited for Elsa to arrive, I pondered how I could establish in her heart the same kind of bank account my grandparents created in me—to pay it forward so she will know fifty years from now that her Mia loved her fiercely.

With hours to play together, we began our sunny afternoon with me pushing her on the swing that hangs from a high, strong cedar branch in our backyard. I told her she looked like a princess with her blonde curls blowing in the breeze. I laughed with joy at her beauty and told her she had learned to pump herself high in the air before her older cousins had. Next we happened upon a baby green frog about a half inch long. We made diving boards for him to jump into the baby pool. After we gave Jumpy his freedom back, Elsa sang and danced under the dogwood tree while I prepared make-believe pizza and ice cream sundaes in the blue-and-white playhouse. When we tired of the outdoors, Elsa chose four books for me to read. We sat on the front-porch swing with quilts and pillows, and I read the books to her that I had once read to her father.

One of the other favorite things we do when our grandchildren come over is create maps of places the children have traveled to on vacations. We sprawl out all over the floor and draw the mountain ranges of Colombia or the water surrounding Madagascar. The school teacher in me loves the learning and chaos. It's so much fun (and so hard to clean up afterward with a body that gets much more tired in a day than it used to!). We also build forts out of cardboard boxes and construct fire trucks and trains with egg cartons and Crayons. Outside, the children choose climbing trees or shrubs as their rightful homes and fiercely protect their "kingdoms." We take walks through the forest and find treasures that I often previously hid. We sing together in the hammock and watch the clouds go by and the eagles soar.

I've changed many things in our home to please and accommodate our grandchildren. I turned the study off Dan's and my bedroom into their bedroom and playroom. I painted four bright folk-art angels and hung them on the wall above the two-hundred-year-old trundle bed that my son once slept in. The paintings are quite large and take up the space from the headboard to the ceiling. Each angel holds a different object. There is the fierce angel with gladiator clothing and armor holding a shiny sword. His wings are huge and shining gold, and he stands on a hill with sheep all around him. He is the angel who protects the flock. We draw our little ones' attention to him at night when they miss their home and their parents.

There is also an angel with red cowboy boots and a crown of blue flowers on her head. Her wings are white, red, and blue, and the red sash around her dress blows in the wind. A large fish is dangling from her left hand.

Painting by Becky Allender

The sky and the ground swirl with light, and a river of life flows behind her. She is the angel who brings the power of the gospel message to us. We explain to our grandchildren that she represents how we must receive the hope of the gospel into our whole being.

The third angel has huge flowers all around her, and puffy pink clouds float above her wings. She holds a large platter of fruit and vegetables and has the sweetest smile of all the angels. People say she looks like me, but I didn't have that in mind when I painted her! Her wings are light orange and speckled with small yellow dots. This angel represents the bounty of good gifts we have now and will have in the future.

The fourth angel is totally different from the others. She stands in red, wild grass holding a huge dove, which represents the Holy Spirit, the third person of the Trinity, who resides within everyone who believes that Jesus is the resurrected Son of God. Because Jesus lives, we believe that one day all things will be new, and we'll live and reign in a new kingdom. The new heavens and earth will be established, and we will have eternal life. The blue sky behind the angel is filled with streaks that look like wind, and her eyes are wide with surprise. She stands sideways and looks ready for unexpected things. Our journeys are like that. They are wild and unpredictable at times, and it's good to have an angel (and grandparents!) watching over us.

What is an embrace that will last a lifetime? Is it just the physical arms that enfold us? I imagine that I received less than one hundred embraces from my grandparents in my lifetime, while I've already given my grandchildren thousands. But is it the number that matters? Or is it the love that extends far beyond numbered weekends of care?

I hope that when my grandchildren are older, they'll remember the very simple times we spent together and their angels watching over them. I hope they'll remember feeling seen and heard and will feel grounded in the love that once was and still remains. I hope they will hold on to the custom-designed needlepoint pillows I made for them with their names on them. I ponder whether or not their pillows will accompany them to college or end up in their own children's bedrooms one day.

As their lives continue to change in ways I cannot imagine now, I pray that the love, joy, and hope I have in Jesus will be theirs as well. I hope they will retrieve priceless riches from the bank of love I fill now with my heart and time. I hope that my love will somehow give them ballast when their days are uncertain or filled with worry. And I hope that they will one day pay it forward to the next generation.

QUESTIONS TO PONDER

Listen for echoes of your story in this essay and write about it in your journal. Then ponder the following questions and record your thoughts.

1. If you're a grandparent, what is the primary way you create goodness for your grandchildren?
2. How did your grandparents create goodness for you?
3. What tangible expressions of love and goodness are you creating for your children and grandchildren, nieces and nephews?

Bearing Witness

I awakened to a symphony of foghorns. The earth was filled with thick gray fog, and the thermometer registered in the twenties when I began brewing my morning tea. I noticed the weather a lot more when I was scheduled to be on a city street until 2:30 a.m. That day, the sun peeked through the clouds for a total of forty-nine seconds. I knew this because on socked-in, dark days, a burst of light warrants stopping everything and running to a window.

When I left the house at 5:30 to park and walk to the 6:30 ferry, it was a crisp, moist night but not raining. Wonderful. My watch had quit working, and I feared that I was late. I began running—a woman dressed completely in black, dashing across dark streets. What was I thinking? Oh well, next week I would remember a blinking light to clip to my hat.

Shortly after I walked into the Late Night Outreach office, Esther and Woodleigh arrived, and we were told that our format from now on would be praying first and then loading the carts. Esther, our team leader, read from Lamentations 2:19 to open our prayer time:

Arise, cry out in the night,
    as the watches of the night begin;
pour out your heart like water
    in the presence of the LORD.
Lift up your hands to him
    for the lives of your children,
who faint from hunger
    at every street corner.

Then she read Isaiah 62:6–7:

I have posted watchmen on your walls, O Jerusalem;
    they will never be silent day or night.
You who call on the LORD,
    give yourselves no rest,
and give him no rest till he establishes Jerusalem
    and makes her the praise of the earth.

We began praying, by name, for the women we might see that night. We prayed for the young mothers and their children. We prayed that the women would find jobs and accept our offers to connect them with training facilities that could help liberate them from the traps they were in. We prayed for their lives to change and their dreams to be realized. We prayed that their children, who saw things children shouldn't see, would be shielded from harsh realities. We prayed that the women would see the violence of what they were experiencing and be repulsed by it. We prayed that this revulsion would lead them into the arms of a loving heavenly Father who saw them and called them His beloved. We prayed for safety, since our city had been besieged with violent killings as well as sting operations against pimps and prostituted women and girls.

Late night Outreach in Seattle

At the end of our prayer time, a teammate called to tell us that Tina, the woman she had been mentoring for the past eighteen months, had left the track and was employed and going to school. We cheered at the timing as we began putting on our extra layers. The five of us admitted to being tired and not wanting to go out on the streets that night. It was a worthy battle, but it was dark out there!

When we got to our corner, several women were waiting for hot drinks and supplies. Woodleigh had brought her signature chocolate shavings and whipped cream for the hot chocolate. I was freezing already and wished that I had worn ski pants like Woodleigh had. *Come on,* I chided myself. *Be grateful it's not snowing.* The night had officially begun whether I was dressed properly or not.

The first woman I talked with was wearing an obscenely short red skirt that exposed her buttocks. But she was pretty in her pigtails and surprised me when she initiated a conversation.

"I hate being out here," she told me. "I hate it every time I come out." She went on without prompting. "I do this because the job I used to have didn't pay the bills."

We ended up talking together for almost ten minutes, and I found out that she had two daughters, twelve and fourteen years of age, who were attending private schools. They were on the honor roll and already researching scholarships they could apply for. She was working the streets to pay for their education.

It would all be worth it, she said, if they got to go to college. She still hated what she was doing, but because she loved her children more, she did what she did. This woman wasn't dreaming for herself yet, but she certainly was living for the dreams she had for her girls. And yes, she'd love some hot chocolate with whipped cream and chocolate shavings, and thank you so much for being out here with us tonight.

As the night wore on, I got colder and colder. I couldn't help asking what time it was—something I try not to do. Once I started asking, the night seemed to slow to a crawl. Better to just jump up and down when my feet got numb. (Of course, looking cool was not our agenda!) I decided to treat myself to a homemade Rice Krispies square. My favorite! How long had it been since I'd had one? Memories of my children's birthday celebrations at school were in every crunchy bite. Yum. I could make it through the night. Certainly this would keep me going.

Not long after I finished the entire treat, which had been wrapped festively in wax paper and ribbon, a young teenager came for food and drink and asked for a homemade treat. Well, no more Rice Krispies squares. Oh, me. The young mother who baked for us faithfully each Friday night didn't make an unlimited supply. So now I felt even worse. How fleeting comfort can be.

Queen, a beautiful nineteen-year-old barely woman, came by to show us her new dress. She was freezing and was happy to stand by our heater. She briefly took off her coat so we could see her lovely new outfit. We complimented her on how beautiful she looked and asked how her one-year-old daughter was doing.

She loved to talk about her daughter, no less so than any mother does. We delighted in her daughter and asked if we could see a photo of her. Queen handed us a photo, and we weren't surprised to see that she was beautiful, just like her mother. Queen's daughter was a few weeks younger than my grandson. If I could have found my iPhone seven layers beneath the surface of my clothing, I would have loved to show her a picture of him.

Queen and I were different and yet so alike. I pictured her arriving home closer to the time I would be waking up. I'm grateful that I don't work the streets, but if my circumstances thirty years ago had been the same as our girls', would I have been so different? And who would have borne witness to my suffering?

Sometimes I had to tell myself to quit thinking about the pain I saw on the streets. To ponder the violence against our gender was a train of thought that could keep me awake half the night. And yet if I turned away from thinking about these girls, was there anyone to bear witness to their lives? Who would care? Who would pray?

I knew for a fact that girls and women involved in the sex trade feel invisible and forgotten by our society. Now that I had seen their plight up close, how could I turn away? No, I had to see them and serve them. I had to pray fiercely and claim God's protection over all of the exploited girls throughout this city, state, nation, and world. God had called me to be a watchman of the night. What I was watching was unfortunately not out of the ordinary, and yet, what did I know of this before my nights of outreach? Nothing. I really knew nothing.

K nowing the truth changed me profoundly. All these years later, my heart continues to burn with passion for the release and re-demption of every child, woman and man caught in the complex web of abuse and exploitation. Some nights standing on the street corner in downtown Seattle, I felt as if I was doing so little, and yet I was always praying for our girls and bearing witness to their plight. It is still my privilege to hold these dear girls' faces and names before the throne of my Father, pleading again and again that they will come to know His loyal love.

QUESTIONS TO PONDER

Listen for echoes of your story in this essay and write about it in your journal. Then ponder the following questions and record your thoughts.

1. Who is a witness to your life? What does that person see and fail to see about you?

2. How has reading about the lives of prostituted women made you more aware of how blessed you are and how much you've been given? What are some of the blessings you've experienced in life?

3. As others observe your life, what goodness do you think they see? What blessings would they say you possess?

The Foolishness of God

Friday afternoon the wind picked up, and by dinner time the rain had begun. Darkness fell, and I began packing the layers of clothing that would be required for a cold and soggy evening, wondering if standing on a street corner handing out condoms and kindness would do any good. I would be crazy not to question and wonder. It wasn't as if we saw a lot of women who wanted to use our scholarship and counseling services so they could leave the streets and get different jobs.

My husband drove me to the ferry, and I told him how stupid and foolish I felt for leaving the warmth of our home and heading to the streets. There were moments when I didn't think I could stand there for one more hour and watch broken humanity cry out for justice and redemption while all I could do was pour another drink. I wasn't sure what I thought Dan would say, but the words he chose were the perfect balm for my soul.

"Whenever we do something gospel-oriented, we feel foolish," he said. "Why bother? What good will these hours do?" In fact, he said that in his thirty years of speaking about the scourge of sexual abuse, he always wondered whether his words would make a difference. Did a message about God's love and His power to heal and redeem sometimes sound ridiculous to those whose hearts had been battered by evil?

My husband's honest words helped me take heart. Feeling like my "help" was weak at best and pointless at worst was an inevitable part of the battle I entered. I wouldn't feel shame for despairing thoughts but recognized the cunning way evil worked to keep me hopeless and disengaged when I felt powerless.

After talking with Dan, I was fortified and grateful and ready to go. I ferried in the dark, walked a mile of city streets, and after praying, worked with our team to load the van with three large thermoses of hot water, a heater, medical supplies, homemade heart-shaped cookies, and scarves and gloves and condoms and candy. Women were already waiting for us when we got to our corner.

Since the night was slower than normal, I had time to talk with a coworker. She told me about Tara, who had gone to an in-patient rehab facility ten times over the past few years. Even though she had received counseling and care, she always returned to drugs and her life on the streets. It was disturbing to hear of this young woman's unsuccessful attempts to reintegrate into society. It's easy to lose hope of making a difference when people's stories are so heavy with despair. Suddenly I felt again like a church lady speaking into a world I barely comprehended. Teaching a "safe" Bible study seemed to make more sense for someone like me.

What does it mean to live with hope and do so as one who knows the foolishness of God? One of the passages in Scripture that has always moved me is the apostle Paul's description of God's divine foolishness:

Where is the wise person? Where is the teacher of the law? Where is the philosopher of this age? Has not God made foolish the wisdom of the world? For since in the wisdom of God the world through its wisdom did not know him, God was pleased through the foolishness of what was preached to save those who believe. Jews demand signs and Greeks look for wisdom, but we preach Christ crucified: a stumbling block to Jews and foolishness to Gentiles, but to those whom God has called, both Jews and Greeks, Christ the power of God and the wisdom of God. For the foolishness of God is wiser than human wisdom, and the weakness of God is stronger than human strength. (1 Corinthians 1:20–25)

I demand signs. I look for wisdom that makes sense. But I haven't been able, through my wisdom or the wisdom of the ages, to describe the unutterable or to utter the indescribable. It would make more sense for God to have put His message into the hands and mouth of an angel with a flaming sword. The word might still be rejected, but the imposing presence of an angel would at least be difficult to ignore. Instead, He put His word into the hands of a multilayered, raincoat-covered church lady who offered kindness and cocoa to prostituted women. If that wasn't foolish, it was at least ridiculous. Even I felt shocked when I saw myself in the mirror, and yet I couldn't help but go out in the rain. I had to speak, or the fire inside would burn.

"Hope deferred makes the heart sick," Proverbs 13:12 says, "but a longing fulfilled is a tree of life." Hope is a precious commodity. It's like a ninety-year-old grandmother planting an oak tree in her yard. It takes great faith and strength to dig that hole and see beyond the scope of her life to take such a grand action. Without a lifetime of seeing the goodness of the Lord in the land of the living, why would that grandmother be foolish enough to plant an oak tree? And why would a grandmother make the trek from her island home to walk city streets until 2:30 am in the morning? Because I had to do something that said, "Not on my watch!"

For me, all hope is tied to the resurrection, the promise that Jesus is the firstfruits of the promise of God to restore all things. The resurrection is the radical disruption of everything we know. Death is inevitable; it ends everything we know to be good. The dead do not speak. But one did. His promise to raise us into the fullness of His glory is, as C. S. Lewis observed, the words of a charlatan, a madman, or the Son of God who was raised from the dead.

I choose to trust in the latter. It was enough to get me out on the streets on Friday nights, still feeling foolish but prepared to call the foolishness of God wiser than the wisdom of men.

QUESTIONS TO PONDER

Listen for echoes of your story in this essay and write about it in your journal. Then ponder the following questions and record your thoughts.

1. Have you ever risked being foolish for God? If so, what happened? If not, what obstacles do you need to overcome to take this risk?
2. In what relationship does it feel most ridiculous to live out the foolishness of God?
3. Write about a time when sorrow tempted you to doubt the reality of heaven, where your tears will be wiped away, and everything will be made new.

Strength for the Battle

After my parents died, I went home to Ohio to help clear out their home so we could sell it. They built the house in 1962, and since they had been children during the Great Depression, many things had been carefully saved.

My heart skipped a beat when I opened a drawer and found my dad's World War II diary. He had shown it to me the summer before he died, telling me that it was against military policy to have a diary during the war. It made sense that diaries could give the enemy important military secrets if found. He described how he had to write clandestinely and keep it hidden. I was shocked to realize that he had purposely broken the law. I wish I had sat for hours listening to him reflect on his past and asked questions. But my children were more excited about going to the water park with their cousins, so we spent only a short time with his diary.

My father, along with most fathers I knew when I was growing up, rarely talked about the war. I had a vague understanding that he was first stationed on a navy destroyer in the Atlantic, and after special sonar training, he spent the rest of his service on wooden mine sweepers. He also took part in five invasions in North Africa and the Mediterranean.

Becky's dad at the train station during WWII

By the time I was born in the early 1950s, our country had moved on to prosperity, and the trauma of those who had fought for freedom had been neatly boxed up and shelved. Television shows like *Hogan's Heroes* and *McHale's Navy* comprised my childhood understanding of World War II. But at bedtime, my dad would sometimes tell exciting navy stories. Once a mine exploded, and the mine sweeper caught on fire! My father clambered to rescue the radio and remained on the sinking ship, which was going up in flames. The captain hollered instructions to my dad on what to do to save his life and the radio. I remember wondering if I would meet that captain in heaven someday and thank him.

Now that I had a second chance to read my dad's diary, I took the time while my brother and sister were sorting through other items. As I read his description of maritime battles, I experienced a swirl of emotions. Each page was in Technicolor. Bombs streaked across the sky like fireworks, booms piercing my ears, and I could smell the sulfur and hear the screams of young men jumping off mine sweepers to their deaths. How did a twenty-year-old endure all of that? Why had I not heard most of this while I was growing up? Had my dad never spoken to my mom about it? It seems that if he had, my mother would have told me. But he never even mentioned the five invasions he had participated in until after Tom Brokaw honored "the greatest generation" in his television documentary. I imagine that my dad yearned to have been recognized like other veterans who were interviewed on TV. As I look back, I realize that when he brought out his diary to show me, he might have been reaching out to talk—finally talk—about the trauma he had buried so long ago.

Throughout my life, my father would sometimes rage. He was extremely opinionated and seldom tolerated opposing views. When the Vietnam War was in full swing, he couldn't understand why my generation protested and refused to fight. What I know now is that unresolved trauma can damage us emotionally when it resurfaces. In retrospect, I realize that my dad's hair-trigger temper was likely connected to things no young man ought to ever observe, let alone experience. Page after page of his diary became a window into his hidden suffering and a treasure hunt into his heart and its vault full of pain.

When World War II ended, many soldiers were told to find their way home however they could. My father wrote about hitchhiking through Italy to France and then catching a ride on a ship back to the United States. He told about a bombed museum in France where he grabbed two French dueling guns and put them in his duffel. I knew about these guns because I had seen them in the back of a shelf in our family room growing up, but I had no idea of their significance. When I chose what to keep from my parents' home, the guns were part of my booty. This was especially odd, since I don't like guns and we don't have any in our home. Of all my father's possessions, why did

I take those? I wondered. But they turned out to be an important icon of my father's journey and, in a circuitous way, my own.

An icon is a physical metaphor for a story that is not to be forgotten. Every Memorial Day and Fourth of July, I display those French dueling guns as a reminder of the high cost of freedom. The guns convey the terror, death, and victory of my dad's five years of hell. They are proof that he lived through it all and made it home alive. I display his guns because I don't want my father's sacrifice to be forgotten—nor his resolve and stealth in taking those icons.

The guns are icons to me as well. I am a warrior, and I fight in my own ways. I'm disgusted with bullies and like to battle against them. My intercessory praying is fierce, and I believe it is a holy calling. Whether it's standing on street corners protecting prostituted girls or bearing witness to people's stories of trauma in small groups, I stand strong against the Evil One. I know that without prayer and courage, I couldn't do it. Standing strong is evidence not of my strength but of the strength I have because of my dad and because of Jesus.

My father is with Jesus now. He knows far better than I do that the unseen war between good and evil continues to rage on this earth. The cost of a good and faithful life is high. Every time I display his French dueling guns, I proclaim the privilege I have to remember sacrifice and live well.

QUESTIONS TO PONDER

Listen for echoes of your story in this essay and write about it in your journal. Then ponder the following questions and record your thoughts.

1. What object or possession in your home best symbolizes your role as a warrior? Why did you choose this object?
2. On what battlefront are you uniquely called to fight?
3. What do you feel when you describe yourself as a warrior called to fight on a particular front? Explain.

Treasuring the Now
and Not Yet

Oh, whoa! I just saw my right hand typing and was struck cold: *Yikes! This is my hand? You've got to be kidding.* This random observation nearly took my breath away. My hand looked exactly like my mother-in-law's hands looked when she was ninety-one. Seriously, I was a bit freaked out!

Just a bit ago, I was doing yoga with a roomful of young women and felt the energy and vitality around me. The music, the peppermint aromatherapy on my collarbone, the enlivening that comes from stretching, balancing, and breathing in ninety-five-plus-degree heat. Joy and gratefulness accompanied me home. But now, this wrinkled hand with blue, protruding veins confronted me with a different reality: I am way past halfway to heaven!

This isn't the first time this week I've seen the truth about my aging body. I just went for my annual physical, in dread of facing other perceived flaws. I understand why the Beatles wrote a song with the lyrics, "Will you still need me, will you still feed me, when I'm sixty-four?"[4] This year has been my demise in more ways than I care to name. But to name one more, my body seems to have softened and shifted even though I'm eating and exercising the same. It isn't fair! I don't like extra weight around my middle, and I don't want to buy new clothes.

When I was weighed, to my surprise I had gained only one pound since last year. What? It felt (and looked) like ten or fifteen pounds.

I love my primary-care physician. She is beautiful, brilliant, and thorough, and she listens well. She explained that other women my age gain a bit of weight, but it isn't as noticeable. "You are narrow in the middle," Jillian added, "so you can see the weight easily." She went on to say that women tend to remember their younger bodies and expect to stay that way. "When you look at your daughters and daughter-in-law who are thin, it's hard to not remember that your body was once like theirs. But it's time to accept a flabbier stomach." (She didn't use that word, but that's how I interpreted it.)

I think our bodies start to go downhill at about age twenty-seven, but at twenty-seven I didn't feel as if I was going downhill. I was just beginning to have babies, and so much life and goodness were ahead. Now it seems like the best is over—if I choose to stop at the sight of my right hand or fail to offer myself kindness and care regardless of what I see as far from perfect now.

A few years ago, our son and his family lived in Albania. This country was under Communist rule until 1992. During our travels to other Communist countries, Dan and I noticed that people rarely looked one another in the eyes as they passed. Strangers were dangerous and might report your family to the authorities. But in Albania, the expressions on people's faces are welcoming, and the hospitality is bountiful.

While visiting Albania, we learned about the heroic role the Albanians played during World War II. Not a single Jew was turned over to the Italian army during the occupation. Rather than hiding the Jews in attics or barns as many people did during that time, the Albanians gave them documentation and Albanian names. Most important, they treated them like family members. The Albanians saved more than two thousand Jews from Nazi persecution!

This remarkable assistance grew out of a code of honor called *besa* that is unique to being Albanian. It literally means "to keep the promise." Those who act according to *besa* keep their word and offer safety to guests and their families.

Pondering *besa* caused me to think about how often I refuse to offer hospitality, kindness, and safety to myself. It's more natural for me to punish myself for my flaws.

As I moved on to the dreaded mammogram torture chamber at my doctor's office, I practiced welcoming this aging body with a *besa* code of honor: "Thank you, aging arms that bruise easily and have lost so much collagen this year without hormone replacement therapy. You're safe with me. Thank you, eyes, that can't read without glasses. I have seen many amazing sights because of you. Thank you, hair, that is getting whiter each year. I will still make you beautiful."

As I drove home, I continued aloud: "I treasure you, my aging and failing body. We're in this together. You are a gift to me. Even as you become fluffier and droopier, I will be intentional about welcoming you with safety and care."

Later that day I texted a photo to my husband. He was running with our young granddaughter, Elsa, and the slanted, golden sunrays on a gorgeous October day warmed their smiles and curls as they played. He texted back that he looked awful in the photo. I never would have sent it if that had been what I saw. What he saw was an overweight sixty-four-year-old. What I saw was the dearest love of my life who adores his grandchildren and loves his family well.

Becky and Dan on an Hawaiian beach

What does God see when He looks at me? Surely not my swelling midriff and flabbier thighs. I think the parts of me I consider so flawed are actually precious in His sight. That was true for my husband when we were in high school. For some reason Dan loved the very part of my body I loathed. I admired athletic legs, and I had a plan every summer to bicycle up McCoy hill to increase the size of my calves. I did bicycle (not the hundred times I always hoped to pedal) up the hill, but my calf muscles never made the grade, and I always felt less lovely because of my skinny legs. So, isn't it funny that without my knowledge, a classmate loved those skinny legs so much that he dropped his pencil to see them? I never knew that until after I was married, and it continues to be a reminder that what I see as undesirable, God often uses for His purposes.

When I was in high school, I never contemplated getting old. I looked ahead to new experiences, exciting milestones, an abundance of time to go after anything I wanted in life. Four decades later, I'm learning to anticipate things that are far more important than my youthful aspirations. I'm looking ahead to a season of trusting in ways I have never had to trust before.

I'm learning to rely on God's strength with an aging body, to embrace a new way of living that requires more grace to keep going. I'm learning to exchange my critical inward glare for Jesus's joyous delight in me. I practice listening to my body and being kind to it. I am developing a new appreciation for what has been and a more nuanced anticipation of what will be.

You see, it's all new ahead, even with a body that's fading away. For the remaining days of my life, I will cling to the hope of what is not seen. C. S. Lewis referred to the "shadowlands,"[5] where the seen is real, but not the most real. There is something truer beneath the surface that hints at its existence without demanding to be seen. It's like an impression or a scent that cannot be named, yet it cannot be entirely ignored either. This unseen reality will one day come into its full glory. There will be a new heaven and a new earth, as Jesus promised, and all things will be made new. Even these wrinkled hands.

QUESTIONS TO PONDER

Listen for echoes of your story in this essay and write about it in your journal. Then ponder the following questions and record your thoughts.

1. Are you keeping the *besa* code of honor with regard to your body? Explain.
2. What one thing do you find most undesirable about yourself and long to see restored one day in heaven? How does God see that part of you?
3. What three people are you most excited about seeing in heaven? Why?

I Am Not Finished!

"**I** am not finished!" Elsa stomped her foot. We were watching *Mary Poppins*, and Jane, Michael, Bert, and Mary Poppins were on their merry-go-round horses galloping off into the spring meadow. It's a glorious moment in the film, but my sweet two-and-a-half-year-old granddaughter had come to the end of the thirty minutes of screen time her parents had allotted. I told her we'd watch more the next day, but that wasn't what she wanted to hear.

After throwing a mini-tantrum, Elsa started quietly rocking in her rocking chair. I was so proud of the way she self-soothed and cared for herself after being so frustrated and disappointed. We soon went on to another activity, but I realized that Elsa's statement had triggered something in me that needed to be processed. Something about that sentence "I am not finished" brought tears to my eyes.

I began thinking of all the moments in my life when I could have said, "I am not finished!" One experience immediately sprang to mind. The summer after I finished my sophomore year in college, I begged my parents to allow me to transfer out of state. I was desperate to flee my boyfriend, who suffered from bipolar disorder before most understood what that meant. He was either abusive or charming as a prince. I had lived through three turbulent years of physical, emotional, and sexual abuse, and looking back, I see how I was bonded to him the way a prostituted woman is bonded to her pimp. Twice I broke up with him, and twice he tried to kill himself. Twice he ended up in psychiatric hospitals. Twice I caved under the weight of holding his life in my hands. Twice I returned to him to save his life. But this time I had to get away.

My parents granted my transfer request, and I started afresh in a new school with a new major and all new friends. I immersed myself in anthropology courses and did really well. I was free. I was alive. I was happy. I applied and was chosen to participate in an archaeological dig in the mountains of western Colorado during summer semester. I was honored to be among fifteen students from all over the country who would do site surveying for Indian relics and remains before oil companies began mining for shale. We worked on remote bluffs and along clear, rushing riverbeds in the most beautiful terrain I had ever seen. Herds of wild horses galloped by, and eagles soared above us each day as the cares of civilization drifted away from my consciousness. As a midwestern girl, I felt as though I were near heaven.

On the last night of the dig, while I was sleeping in a tent with two other girls, my adviser entered and quietly climbed onto my cot. He started kissing me while pulling down his pants, and I could smell the liquor on his breath. I froze and couldn't speak. I couldn't move as he forcibly raped me[6]. I didn't want to embarrass him in front of the other girls. What he was doing horrified me, but at the same time, I felt so ashamed at what was happening to me. I hoped my tentmates had slept through it. Afterward I lay still, barely breathing. I can still hear the sound of his dirty hiking boots scraping the hardened dirt floor of the tent as he climbed through the triangle canvas door flap, never saying a word.

The next morning I showed up for scheduled kitchen duty with my adviser. As I prepared the oatmeal on the camp stove and set the tables, I avoided any eye contact with him. I wondered how I would be able to make it through the next five minutes.

After breakfast we loaded the Jeeps, and I rode away from camp as if nothing had happened. Each of us flew home to different parts of the country, returning to our respective lives. But I was a dead girl walking. I couldn't return to the university and the anthropology classes I had come to love. I couldn't even tell my roommate what had happened. I telephoned her from Ohio and asked her to send home all my belongings on a Greyhound bus, leaving her to find another roommate for the house we had rented. Then I changed my major. It took me fifteen years to call what happened in that tent what it actually was: rape.

I thought that my revenge on what evil had done to me was marrying a man whose calling is to minister to those who have been sexually violated. "What evil intended for harm, God meant for good," I claimed. But after our third child, Andrew, was born, I realized I needed help. When my counselor reminded me that I had been asleep when my adviser crawled on top of me, I was able to name what happened as rape. Years after that, I sat under Dan's teaching and realized that even though I was twenty-one years old at the time, what happened wasn't my fault. Only recently, however, have I experienced healing at the deepest level.

I have my story group to thank. For our deepest traumas, we need more than mere encouragement and empathy to heal. We need someone who will read our stories at a deeper level and pursue the hidden tracks to our hearts.

As I revisited my story of rape and shame and shared it with my group, our group leader said to my peers who were trying to enter the sadness, "What did you most notice in Becky's story?" My group cared for me well, but our brilliant leader named something that the group did not. The focus had been on the horror and heartbreak of the rape itself. That is understandable. But what the leader pointed out to the group was where my heart seemed to be most alive and passionate while I read my story. She asked my peers to consider where in the narrative I seemed most free.

I had written, "Fifteen college students from other universities along with two professors set off for six weeks of site surveying for Indian relics in the most beautiful setting imaginable. The herds of wild horses galloping by and eagles soaring overhead were otherworldly to an Ohio girl. It was as close to heaven as I had ever been."

I had spoken those sentences with my eyes almost closed, breathing deeply and remembering the beauty of the time and place in the Rocky Mountains. I have no clue how our story-group leader knew to enter that doorway. She said, "Didn't you see her? Didn't you feel her freedom? Didn't you hear her say that after three years in an abusive relationship, she finally left Ohio? Didn't you get how hard that was, and then weren't you there with her when she spoke of the eagles and the wild horses?"

My group pursued my story more deeply, naming other places where I had buried my dreams and lost the passion that once had been so alive in me.

They took me back to the horror of a "dead girl walking" and comforted me in the moment when I changed my major and gave up what I had loved so dearly.

Becky in college

After we all returned to our homes, I was swept up in my usual busyness and didn't reflect any further on the losses that had been named. A month later, Elsa's sentence triggered my tears. "I am not finished." I was not finished. I had not fully mourned the wild horses I had lost.

Sometimes people ask, "Why go back to sad places in your life?" It isn't an easy question to answer convincingly when someone believes it's wrong or useless to return to sorrow. All I can say is that in sorrow and in the care of wise guides, stories of brokenness become holy as we taste the tears of God. The experience is life changing. Research even shows that our brains actually change when we tell stories of loss in a safe setting and receive care.

As I've continued to process my losses and my grief, the puzzle of who I am and who I'm meant to be unfolds with resurrection hope, even at sixty-five years of age. I have felt the Father's delight and love in renewed ways. There is so much more to my story than I thought, and there is so much more tenderness from Jesus to experience. I hear my Savior say with a bold, fierce twinkle in His eye, "I was not finished!" And He isn't. He who died for me and said, "It is finished" once and for all invites me to a new, wild, freeing life. I am not finished, and apparently neither are Elsa and Jesus. I am not finished!

I am not finished!

QUESTIONS TO PONDER

Listen for echoes of your story in this essay and write about it in your journal. Then ponder the following questions and record your thoughts.

1. What major obstacles did you face as a young adult?
2. What dreams did you have to let go of? Why did those dreams not work out?
3. What new dreams were birthed out of heartache in your life?

REFERENCES

1. Neha A. Deshpande and Nawal M. Nour, "Sex Trafficking of Women and Children," *Reviews in Obstetrics and Gynecology* 6, no. 1 (2013): 22–27, www.ncbi.nlm.nih.gov/pmc/articles/PMC3651545/.
2. Joy DeGruy, *Post Traumatic Slave Syndrome: America's Legacy of Enduring Injury and Healing* (Portland, OR: Joy DeGruy Publications, 2005), marketing summary.
3. Kim Simon, "To My Fellow Moms on the First Day of Kindergarten," *The Blog, Huffington Post*, August 21, 2014, www.huffingtonpost.com/kim-simon/to-my-fellow-moms-on-the-first-day-of-kindergarten_b_5693541.html.
4. John Lennon and Paul McCartney, "When I'm Sixty-Four," *Sgt. Pepper's Lonely Hearts Club Band*, copyright 1967 Capitol Records.
5. *Shadowlands*, directed by Richard Attenborough (Price Entertainment, 1993).
6. Grace Galliano et al., "Victim Reactions during Rape/Sexual Assault: A Preliminary Study of the Immobility Response and Its Correlates," Journal of Interpersonal Violence 8, no. 1 (March 1993): 109–14.

ABOUT THE AUTHOR

Becky Allender graduated from the Ohio State University in 1974 with a bachelor of science in elementary education and taught kindergarten before raising three children. In 1998, she earned her master's degree in curriculum and instruction at Colorado Christian University and taught sociology at Colorado Institute of Art to help support their family while Dan established the Seattle School of Theology and Psychology.

Becky has a heart for the sexually exploited and volunteered with Late Night Outreach on the streets of Seattle in 2008 and 2009, offering hot chocolate, compassion, and hugs to prostituted teens and women. She cofounded the Allender Center at the Seattle School in 2010 and directs intercession at the center for certificate training in trauma and abuse. She also leads story workshop groups and coleads marriage retreats with her husband.

Becky and Dan live on Bainbridge Island in Washington State. She loves being a wife, mother, and grandmother and is grateful for the opportunity of getting to know so many of Dan's students and their families over the years.

70057773R00138

Made in the USA
Lexington, KY
08 November 2017